SINGAPORE

First Edition, 2017
Updated, 2018
Lost Guides
www.thelostguides.com

Author
Anna Chittenden

Photographer
Anna Chittenden

Editing & Proofreading
Camilla Lindberg Christensen
Elly Whittaker
Emma Harding
Simren Priestley

Designer
Sarah and Schooling

Map Illustrator
HyunJu Song

Cover Image
Hosanna Swee

Printed and bound in Singapore by Markono Print Media Pte Ltd

MIX
Paper from
responsible sources
FSC™ C009578
www.fsc.org

ISBN 978-981-11-1909-5

Work with Lost Guides
Lost Guides is able to deliver bespoke travel guides and custom
content for your business in both print and digital formats. If you like
what we do, please email *hello@thelostguides.com*

Stock this book
If you are interested in stocking *Lost Guides – Singapore*, please email
hello@thelostguides.com

Also available in this series:
Lost Guides – Bali & Islands
Lost Guides – Tokyo & Beyond

SINGAPORE

A UNIQUE, STYLISH AND OFFBEAT
TRAVEL GUIDE TO SINGAPORE

LOST GUIDES

1ST EDITION

ANNA CHITTENDEN

Contents

Interviews

Literature

Author's Notes

Singapore is one of those cities that can be hard for a visitor to crack. When planning a trip to destinations such as Rome or New York, you might already know where to go - maybe you've seen it in a movie or heard it in a song. For Singapore, I had no such prior knowledge. Now after months of exploring, researching and interviewing, I feel pretty happy that I get to share this city's awesome finds, some that visitors might never otherwise come across.

I've met a silversmith hidden away in a second floor flat on the East Coast pounding out chunky wedding rings, seen a field full of birds singing in their cages on top of lofty poles in Kebun Baru, eaten modern Singaporean cuisine in an old black and white house in a tropical garden, and wandered through a lush jungle with monkeys swinging from branch to branch. I hope you enjoy your visit to Singapore as much as I have enjoyed creating this guide!

What's in the guide?

This book highlights over 120 of the most special spots in Singapore where I love to spend my time. Recommendations include cool coffee shops, authentic Asian art galleries, fabulous food (both local and contemporary), speakeasy bars and boutique hotels. Designed to be practical and provide a unique insight into Singapore, this book is organised into 10 neighbourhoods accompanied by bespoke maps and original photography.

I've also spoken to some of the most inspiring local creatives who are profiled in the book, and some of Singapore's most promising writers have contributed beautiful pieces of literature about this little island.

How did I choose what would go in the book?

I'm drawn to small and intimate places, where the owner might greet you at the door, and you can feel their hard work and passion running through every aspect of the business. I'm also curious about the past and like to find those nuggets of nostalgia - be it a jungle hike, where I imagine wild tigers prowling through the palm trees, or seeing an Uncle expertly throwing together plates of char kway teow, the one and only dish he has been serving since he was a teenager, six or so decades ago.

All of the recommendations that appear in this book are here because they are great! I haven't accepted commissions or payments to feature places in this guide – I simply write about what I love.

Who is this book for?

Lost Guides - Singapore has been created for today's traveller - the stylish nomad with an interest in experience rather than expense and an eye for quality, design and authenticity.

About the Author

Hello! I'm Anna and I'm the author, photographer and explorer behind this book *Lost Guides – Singapore*. I founded my travel website thelostguides.com in 2014 as I was frustrated with the lack of useful and trustworthy information about the places I wanted to visit. I now use this space to share unique and inspiring travel experiences in Asia with the aim of making your travel planning that little bit easier!

In November 2015 I launched my first book *Lost Guides – Bali*, which has been recommended by Condé Nast Traveller and Travel & Leisure. The updated second edition, *Lost Guides – Bali & Islands*, was launched in March 2018. During 2018 I'll be spending time in Japan to carry out research for my next book *Lost Guides – Tokyo* which will be out in 2019. The books are stocked in some awesome shops like BooksActually in Singapore, Stanfords in London, Periplus in Indonesia, and online on Amazon.

Drop me a line

Your feedback is really important to me. I'd love to know your thoughts on the book, as well as any suggestions or hidden gems you've uncovered on your travels. Please share your lovely photos of your trip with me using the hashtag **#lostguidessingapore**

- ✉ anna@thelostguides.com
- ⊚ @lostguides
- 🐦 @lostguides
- 🅕 Lost Guides

Visit my website **thelostguides.com** to read free online travel guides and to sign up to the newsletter.

Need to Know

Language: Singapore has four official languages: English, Malay, Mandarin and Tamil. The most widely used language is English. Singaporeans also speak a localised dialect of English called Singlish.

Budget: Singapore is an expensive city, so take this into account when planning your stay here. Things like alcohol are expensive, but taxis, public transport and local food are cheap.

Accommodation: Like with any international city, prices for accommodation in Singapore can be high, especially when compared to other Southeast Asian destinations. In this book, I've recommended places with a range of prices, from budget, to mid-range and luxury stays.

Visas: Singapore is visa-free for visitors from countries including those in the European Union, United Kingdom, Australia, United States, Switzerland, Norway and South Korea. Please check the foreign travel advice in your country for up-to-date visa information.

Money: The currency in Singapore is Singapore Dollars (SGD). There are ATMs at the airport and around the city. Most places take card, although you'll need cash for some taxis and smaller businesses.

Transport: Taxis are affordable; the main apps are Grab and Comfort. Public transport is good. The metro train system is called the MRT. Buy an EZ-Link travel card from any MRT station for use on MRTs and buses.

When to go: Singapore has a tropical climate with no distinct seasons. The average temperature is 27°C, and the humidity levels are high. It rains throughout the year, although often only for short periods of time.

Note: in this book, where prices are listed as $ this is Singapore Dollars (SGD).

Pulau Ubin

Tekong Island

Changi Airport

Little India & Jalan Besar

Bugis & Kampong Glam

East Coast

Chinatown & Telok Ayer

Central & Marina Bay

↑ N

Chinatown & Telok Ayer

The Charm of Chinatown

Once Singapore had established its position as Southeast Asia's leading trading post by 1819, ships of migrants set sail from provinces in southern China, such as Fujian and Guangdong, seeking their fortunes. They risked their lives on the long and treacherous journey to the shores of Singapore, each soul in search of a better life. While wealthy merchants prospered trading fine silks, leaves of tea and tobacco and pretty porcelain, a dark underbelly of opium dens, gambling habits and secret societies emerged in the increasingly cramped conditions of Chinatown.

Today, strolling along the "five-foot-way" walkways beside ornately decorated shophouses and along freshly swept pavements, it's hard to imagine such a world existed. Yet the past still quietly breathes through the buildings where these migrants once lived, buildings that were luckily saved from destructive development plans. Though overshadowed by gleaming skyscrapers, these hidden corners of Singapore retain their character and charm. Streets sprinkled with Chinese medicine apothecaries and traditional teahouses now sit alongside hip restaurants and boisterous bars; this mix, with its subtle tension between old and new, is a striking representation of Singapore today.

The Lion City clings to the nostalgia and comfort of yesterday while clawing to be recognised as a modern and forward thinking global city.

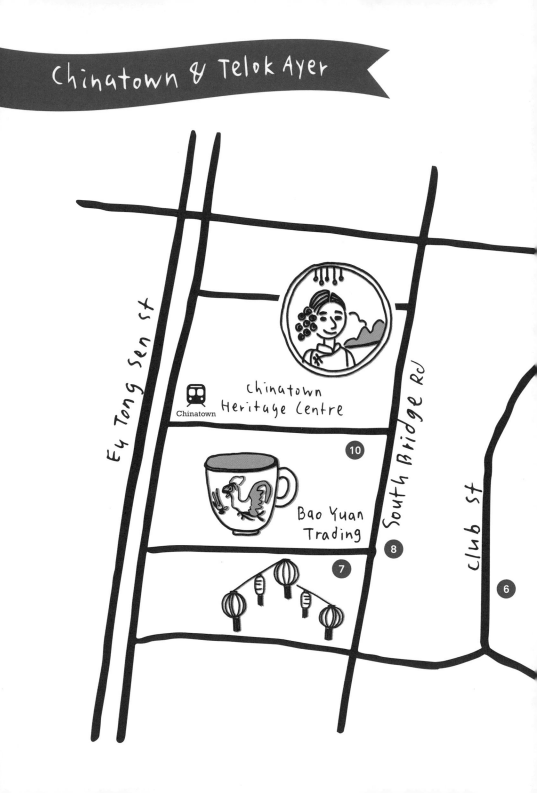

Chinatown & Telok Ayer

Eu Tong Sen St

Chinatown

Chinatown Heritage Centre

Bao Yuan Trading

South Bridge Rd

Club St

10

8

7

6

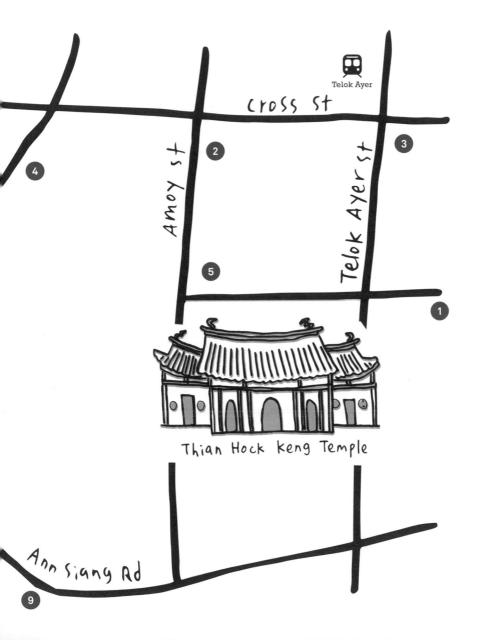

Cheek by Jowl

1 *Modern Australian Marvel*

As well as great food, the magic ingredient that makes a restaurant so special is the friendly and passionate people that run the place. Cheek By Jowl is helmed by husband-and-wife duo, Rishi (the chef) and Manuela (the restaurant manager). They offer a marvellous 'chef's tasting menu', done in a laid-back and casual style. Go for the reasonably priced $88 5-course menu, with delicious dishes such as artichoke with onion consommé, barramundi with charred lettuce and lamb with smoked eggplant. They also do super snacks, like oysters topped with tomato. Manuela is a master with the wine list, suggesting lesser-known organic and biodynamic varieties from boutique vineyards. Grab a counter-top seat so that you can view the chefs in action in the open kitchen.

🏠 21 Boon Tat St, 069620

🚇 Telok Ayer

☎ +65 62211911

↖ cheekbyjowl.com.sg

f Cheek by Jowl

⊙ @cheekbyjowlsg

🕐 Mon – Fri 12pm – 2.30pm, 6pm – 10.30pm
Sat 6pm – 2.30pm
Closed Sun

Ding Dong

2 *Eclectic Asian Flavours*

🏠 115 Amoy St, 069935

🚇 Telok Ayer

☎ +65 65570189

↖ dingdong.com.sg

✉ theteam@dingdong.com.sg

📘 Ding Dong

📷 @dingdongsg

🕐 Mon – Fri 12pm- 3pm, 6 – 12am
Sat 6 – 12am
Closed Sun

A celebration of Southeast Asian flavours, Ding Dong is a fun and fabulous dining spot on the ever so happenin' Amoy Street. Walls are plastered with retro oriental posters, while the seats are like multi-coloured Smarties sweets. The chef takes inspiration from traditional dishes from the neighbouring countries of Thailand, Malaysia and Vietnam, tinkering and experimenting with modern techniques to create something altogether progressive. Sample the scrumptious small plates such as the Hokkaido scallop tartare wrapped in coconut kuih kapit (like the love letters sent for Chinese New Year!) and the signature 5-spiced lamb tongue. I absolutely love their cocktail creations – my favourite being the 'Hawker' with gin, hawberry, Japanese cucumber and egg white that comes with a side of 1980s Singapore haw flake candy. The set lunch menu is good value, and the ambience is great for dinner too – plus it's near lots of groovy bars on the strip.

Moosehead

3 *Cosy Corner Kitchen*

Moosehead is the shy and unassuming star on Telok Ayer Street, a little restaurant that lets the food do the talking. For those who prefer their feasts to be casual and relaxed, this is the place to go. Run by a Greek-Australian father and son duo, Moosehead takes inspiration from the shores of Europe via foodie Oz. Start with the fried artichoke and ricotta with lemon and radicchio - a fresh and fragrant dish that tastes as good as it looks. The roast cauliflower, garlic miso and leek confit is surprisingly hearty, and the beetroot, sumac yogurt, spiced ponzu and almonds is another awesome veggie option. A signature dish is the crispy-spiced pig's ears – tastier than it sounds! – and the sharing plates make Moosehead great for small groups. This restaurant offers a quirky take on comfort food in a cool, laidback environment.

🏠 110 Telok Ayer St, 068579

🚊 Telok Ayer

☎ +65 66368055

↖ mooseheadproject.com

✉ eatdrinkshare@mooseheadproject.com

📘 Moosehead Kitchen – Bar

📷 @mooseheadkitchenbar

🕐 Mon – Fri 12pm – 2.30pm, 6 -10.30pm
   Closed Sun

Luke's

4 *Classic American Chophouse*

Contemporary and classy, Luke's is a fabulous restaurant that takes the best of the US and brings it to the sunny shores of Singapore. Masterminded by Chef Travis Masiero, the food on offer is a representation of his heritage and relationships established during his tenure as a chef in the US. He knows exactly where the seafood is from, having visited many of the suppliers himself. Start by ordering oysters from Massachusetts or Maine, and treat yourself to a lobster mac & cheese (the best!). Tuck into table snacks such as tuna tartare with avocado and jumbo shrimp cocktail from the oyster bar. With its high quality food and service, Luke's is a definite treat place. There's also a branch of this restaurant over on Orchard Road, located on the 3rd floor of The Heeren, Robinsons department store.

🏠 22 Gemmill Ln, 069257

☎ +65 62214468

↖ lukes.com.sg

✉ info@lukes.com.sg

f Luke's Oyster Bar & Chop House

📷 @lukesoysterbar

🕐 Mon – Sat 12pm – 12am
Closed Sun

Amoy Street Bars

5 *Quirky Drinking Holes*

Employees Only

Somewhat of an institution in New York where the bar is a go-to for industry insiders, Employees Only has now sprung up in Singapore, serving great cocktails in a small but atmospheric space, decked out in art-deco interiors. This place is always lively when you're looking for a late night tipple.

 112 Amoy St, 069932

employeesonlysg.com

Mon – Sun 5pm – 1am

Jigger & Pony

Taking its name from when cocktails were listed in 'jiggers' and 'ponies' in the 19th century, this is the place to pick up a great Negroni or a strong Old Fashioned, poured over hand-carved ice. Adding a contemporary edge to the line-up are their signature drinks. I love the 'corpse reviver #101' with Babicka Vodka, St Germain, Absinthe jelly and jasmine sweet vermouth.

 101 Amoy St, 069921

jiggerandpony.com

Mon – Thurs 6pm – 1am
Fri – Sat 6pm – 3am
Closed Sun

Native Bar

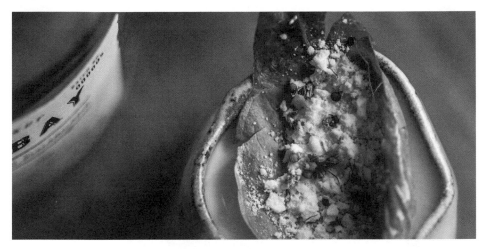

This bar on the 2nd floor of a shophouse on Amoy Street proudly serves quirky cocktails using locally-sourced produce. Using foraged ingredients to flavour the drinks, Native Bar is well known for its 'Antz' cocktail, made with real ants, Thai rum, sugarcane and soursop. Try other regional spirits such as Ceylon Arrack and Indian whisky, mixed with Sri Lankan spices.

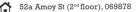

🏠 52a Amoy St (2nd floor), 069878

🕊 tribenative.com

🕐 Mon – Sat 6pm – 12am
Closed Sun

The Spiffy Dapper

Starting off life on Boat Quay, The Spiffy Dapper now resides in a subtle space up some dark stairs on Amoy Street. This no-nonsense bar serves some seriously tasty drinks like 'Sheik on the level' made with black tea gin, lemon juice and egg whites or 'Bee's knees chassis' with pisco and pineapple syrup.

🏠 73 Amoy St (2nd floor), 069892

🕊 spiffydapper.com

🕐 Mon – Fri 5pm – 1am
Sat – Sun 6pm – 1am

Operation Dagger

6 *Theatrical Drinking Den*

A lot of bars on the Club Street stretch are pretty basic in terms of drinks on offer. If bottles of big brand beer and cheap-tasting wine aren't your thing, then sashay on down to the discreet basement drinking-den, Operation Dagger. Dreamt up by Luke Whearty, an Aussie bartender extraordinaire, on first impression it feels like you've stepped into a medieval laboratory, rather than a bar. Apothecary-style bottles filled with home-made spiced rum and caramel tea line the walls, traditional Japanese coffee sieves are used to infuse orange, cinnamon and sake, while honeycomb is thrown into liquid nitrogen for the 'milk + honey' cocktail along with brandy and tonka bean. My favourite cocktail has to be the 'hot + cold' with warm foam on top of a cool pineapple piña colada. In the corner of the basement you may spy a sous vide bath bubbling away, slowly poaching pear, vanilla, curry leaf and burnt sugar for the 'fallen fruit' creation.

🏠 7 Ann Siang Hill, 069791

🚇 Chinatown or Telok Ayer

🖱 operationdagger.com

✉ info@operationdagger.com

📘 Operation Dagger

📷 @lukewookie

🕐 Tues – Sat 6pm – 12am
Closed Sun – Mon

Bao Yuan Trading

7 *Cheerful Chinese Crockery*

Hidden behind the stalls of cheap tourist tat on Temple Street is a row of kitchenware shops selling the best selection of Chinese porcelain in town. This is my go-to place for finding gifts for friends and family back home (pink Peranakan egg cups anyone?), or for filling my kitchen cupboard with fun crockery with character. Come here to stock up on stacks of blue and white koi fish porcelain bowls, pretty patterned plates in turquoise hues and bright yellow paints, as well as bowls made using the traditional rice grain technique. They sell the cutest sake cups and one-off pieces such as chopstick holders in shapes of squid and floundering fish, with prices starting at just a few dollars and small enough to take in your cabin bag home. Old but not strictly antique, it's also a great place to pick up gorgeous tall vases and old-school umbrella stands.

🏠 15 Temple St, 058562

🚇 Chinatown

📞 +65 62271189

✉️ baoyuan@live.com.sg

East Inspirations

8 *Authentic Asian Antiques*

🏠 33 Pagoda St, 059192

☎ +65 62242993

↖ east-inspirations.com

✉ eastinspirations@hotmail.com

📘 East Inspirations

🕐 Mon - Sun 10.30am – 6.30pm

It's easy to want almost everything at East Inspirations, an authentic, family-run Chinese antique shop directly opposite the Sri Mariamman Temple. Marvel at a beautiful 20th century red-painted carved wedding bed with stacked lacquer food carrier boxes used for the same ceremony. Rich orange silks hang from the wall, with detailed embroidery of bold dragons and floral designs. More practical items include lovely Chinese lamps. Choose a vase that you like and they'll transform it into a lamp, adding the electrical parts and lampshade. I'm a little bit obsessed with the ornate small shoes on show, which were worn by women who had their feet bound – once a sign of beauty, this custom was brought over to Singapore by the Chinese community that migrated here. Other favourite items include the now trendy Chinese ceramic garden stools (go here for the real deal).

Ann Siang House

9 *Quirky & Cosy Hotel*

Hotels in Singapore can feel cold and corporate, or worse — shiny and tacky (in the guise of attempted "luxury"). Luckily a few lovely boutique hotels have popped up; many of them housed in restored heritage buildings with character. If you want to be in the centre of the action near Club Street and Amoy Street, then the 20-room hotel, Ann Siang House, is a good choice. The rooms feel homely and comfortable, with splashes of colourful art on the walls (the whole hotel is filled with fab pieces), and deep freestanding bathtubs for a leisurely soak. Fun bars and restaurants are dotted around the hotel. Head up to the rooftop terrace for sunset cocktails at Peruvian themed Tiger's Milk, and grab a bite to eat in the basement from Blue Label Pizza & Wine.

🏠 28 Ann Siang Hill, 069708

🚇 Chinatown or Telok Ayer

☎ +65 62029377

🖊 annsianghouse.com

✉ stay@annsianghouse.com

📘 Ann Siang House

💲 From $250

Chinatown Heritage Centre

10 *Singapore's Stories*

The vibrant but gritty past of Chinatown comes to life within three lovingly restored shophouses on busy Pagoda Street. Using the memories and original artefacts from over 300 residents, life in the 1950s has been recreated to allow visitors to be immersed in Singapore's story. Step inside Tuck Cheong Tailor shop, where European style suits were made for wealthy Chinese businessmen, and hear the humming of the sewing machine against the noise of the radio blasting out tales of Chinese legends. Signs of opium addiction are peppered around the rooms – a vice brought in by the British and used by landlords to attract tenants (until the 1980s, illegal opium dens could still be found in Singapore). I love the physician's room at the front of the house filled with family photos and apothecary pots. The physician's daughter recently shared her own experiences of growing up here as a young girl. Time your trip with the guided tours (at 1.30pm or 4.30pm).

🏠 48 Pagoda St, 059207

🚇 Chinatown

☎ +65 6224 3928

🡥 chinatownheritagecentre.com.sg

📘 Chinatown Heritage Centre

📷 @chinatownheritagecentre

💲 $15, or $20 with guided tour

🕐 Mon - Sun 9am – 8pm
Closed 1st Mon of the month

Thian Hock Keng Temple

11 *Singapore's Sea-goddess Temple*

🏠 158 Telok Ayer St, 068613

🚇 Telok Ayer

↖ thianhockkeng.com.sg

📘 Thian Hock Keng

⊘ Mon – Sun 7.30am – 5.30pm

Sandwiched between the restaurants and bars along Telok Ayer Street, Thian Hock Keng Temple, built in 1839, is a stunning reminder of Singapore's earlier years. Chinese migrants took to sea to venture from their homeland to the shores of this little island. On arrival, they flocked to the temple to offer their prayers and thanksgiving for their safe journey - at the time the temple stood on the beachside, before the reclamation of land. The temple is dedicated to the deity named Mazu, a Chinese sea goddess, and is the oldest and most important temple of the Hokkien people in Singapore today. The temple has been built to reflect traditional southern Chinese architecture and design, featuring intricate carvings and sculptures of dragons and phoenixes. Try and time your visit to coincide with special ceremonies, such as the Chinese New Year celebrations, the Qing Ming Festival (also known as Tomb Sweeping Day) or the birthday of Jade Emperor to see the temple at its most vibrant.

Everton Park & Keong Saik Road

Hip Heritage Hoods

Neighbouring Chinatown to the Southeast, are the two charismatic heritage areas of Keong Saik Road, and Everton Park; both charming in their own right.

In the 1960s, Keong Saik Road was well known as a seedy red-light district, with most of the shophouses lining the street housing brothels. Slowly the road has evolved, with bordellos becoming boutique hotel bedrooms, and trendy restaurants and cocktails bars popping up along the stretch. At the lower end of the street, keep an eye out for the stacks of shoes belonging to those who are worshiping inside the colourful Sri Layan Sithi Vinayagar Temple. This area is also now filled with vegan cafes, co-working spaces and some of Singapore's best restaurants.

Across the road is the Everton Park Estate, a more residential neighbourhood with pockets of small businesses emerging. Marked by bright orange HDB (housing and development board) homes, with avenues of tall green palm trees, hip coffee houses have cropped up beside laundrettes and provision shops. Beautifully preserved heritage homes hold their ground along Everton Road and Blair Road, with marvellous murals by artist Yip Yew Chong depicting Amah's home-made kueh kueh and alleyway barbershops painted on the walls.

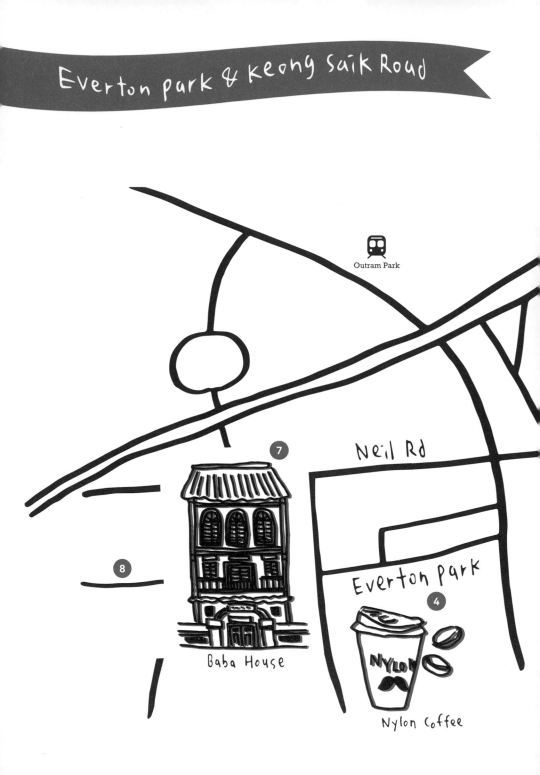

Everton Park & Keong Saik Road

Outram Park

Neil Rd

7

Baba House

8

Everton Park

4

NYLON

Nylon Coffee

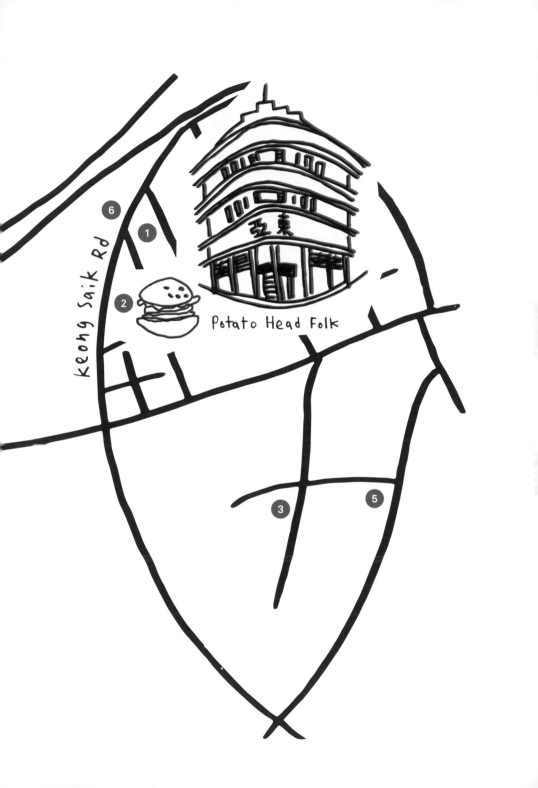

Keong Saik Rd

Potato Head Folk

Burnt Ends

1 *Contemporary Australian BBQ*

During my time in Singapore, Burnt Ends has become one of my all-time favourite restaurants that I return to time and time again. Although often reaching the best restaurants list in Asia (and the world!), for me, Burnt Ends wins for its casual, low-key atmosphere. The restaurant has intimate, communal seating (no fancy white table cloths here) and super friendly chefs that are happy to chat to you while busy preparing your meal. This modern Australian restaurant centres around a four-tonne, dual-cavity, wood-burning machine, giving a whole new meaning to the term BBQ. My top-picks on the menu have to be the smoked quail egg and caviar and the beef marmalade and pickles to start, followed by the king crab plus the bone marrow bun for mains. With only 19 seats, this popular place gets pretty busy so be sure to book well in advance (the first seating is at 6pm).

🏠 20 Teck Lim Rd, 088391

🚇 Outram Park or Chinatown

☎ +65 62243933

↖ burntends.com.sg

📘 Burnt Ends SG

📷 @burntends_sg

🕐 Tues 6pm – 12am
Wed – Sat 11.45am-2pm. 6pm – 12am
Closed Sun and Mon

Potato Head Folk

2 *Rooftop Cocktails & Burger Bites*

You may have heard of the beach club Potato Head set on the shorelines of Seminyak in Bali. Well the club also has a Singapore sister, occupying four floors of a beautiful 1930s pre-war shophouse on Keong Saik Road. Potato Head Folk has something for everyone. On the second floor you will find the burger joint 'Three Buns', a space that feels like you have walked into someone's living room, with low-slung sofas and colourful artwork on the walls. Beware; the burgers, with names like 'Burning Man' and 'Truff Ryder' are dangerously addictive. Don't leave without heading up to the rooftop tiki bar, an airy bohemian oasis with a rum-heavy cocktail menu. For a discreet late night drinking sesh, slip into Studio 1939, a dimly lit space on the third floor.

🏠 36 Keong Saik Rd, 089143

🚇 Outram Park or Chinatown

☎ +65 63271939

↖ ptthead.com

📘 Potato Head Folk

📷 @pttheadsg

🕐 Tues – Sun 11am – 12am
Closed Mon

Lucha Loco

3 *Marvellous Mexican Munch*

🏠 15 Duxton Hill, 089598

🚆 Tanjong Pagar

☎ +65 62263938

↖ luchaloco.com

✉ Lucha Loco

📘 @luchaloco

🕐 Tues – Sat 5pm – 12am
Closed Sun and Mon

The Mexican food trend has well and truly taken over the world. No city is safe from a deluge of margarita-fuelled openings. For all the hype, Lucha Loco gets it really right. I love its location set in a lush green corner of Duxton Hill, and its long turquoise tables lined up on the grass means it's great for groups (I've celebrated many a boisterous birthday here). Lucha Loco's street food inspired menu offers tasty fish tacos and refreshing mango and snapper ceviche and I can't get enough of their elotes (grilled corn on the cob with cotija cheese) and their tostaditas with sirloin. As well as tonnes of tequila choices on the menu, I'm addicted to their passion fruit smashitos with vodka and agave cocktail. Do leave space for their divine desserts – I'm still dreaming about the 'De Chocolate' – warm pistachio and walnut brownie with dark chocolate sauce and crema de mezcal.

Nylon Coffee Roasters

4 *Neighbourhood Micro-Roaster*

🏠 4 Everton Park #01-40, 080004

🚇 Outram Park

↖ nyloncoffee.sg

📘 Nylon Coffee Roasters

📷 @nyloncoffee

🕐 Mon – Fri 8.30am – 5.30pm
Sat – Sun 9am – 6pm
Closed on Tues

There are plenty of cool, trendy coffee shops in Singapore, but none is as unique and unusual as Nylon Coffee Roasters. First up is its location on the ground floor of a bright orange HDB in the Everton Park housing estate with neighbouring businesses including laundromats and barbers. When searching for this hidden hangout, look out for the traditional turquoise sliding doors with simple wooden benches at the front. More than simply running a coffee shop, its founders, Dennis Tang and Jia Min Lee make regular sourcing trips to meet their farmers in far-flung destinations such as Nicaragua or El Salvador for their espresso blend, or Rwanda to source fruity aroma coffee. Watch the roasting action done in-house behind the glass doors of a room named 'The Maillard Project'. A casual joint for a quick cuppa, the coffee shop has tables for standing, and a few chairs dotted around the small room (this isn't a sit here and work on your laptop kinda place).

Six Senses Duxton

5 *Sleek City Retreat*

Six Senses is known for its uber luxurious wellness resorts located in far-flung places such as Yao Noi near Phuket and Laamu in the Maldives, so I was intrigued to hear that they were opening their first city hotel in Singapore. Designed by the much-admired British designer, Anouska Hempel, no detail has been overlooked at this smart, stylish hotel. Quirky and eclectic, it has a rich black and yellow colour scheme, lavishly decorated with sumptuous silk fabrics and dark woods, giving it a distinctly sophisticated Shanghai feel. The 49 rooms have different themes and designs, such as the 'Opium Suite' with a stunning, intricately carved wooden opium bed, and my favourite room, the 'Pearl Suite', with the most gorgeous mother of pearl furniture. As part of their commitment to the surrounding Chinatown community, they've partnered with local independent businesses such as a traditional Chinese medicine physician and a mother-and-daughter-run teahouse for the guests to experience.

🏠 83 Duxton Rd, 089540

🚇 Outram Park or Tanjong Pagar

☎ +65 69141428

↖ sixsenses.com/hotels/duxton

f Six Senses Singapore

⊙ @sixsensessingapore

$ from $400

Hotel 1929

6 *Budget-Friendly Beds*

Finding reasonably priced accommodation in international cities can be a challenge. You want comfort and convenience with a splash of design, but without the hefty price tag. Hotel 1929 ticks all the boxes if you want to be in the mixer, plan to be out and about and don't want to spend over the odds to rest your head. What could be described as a posh hostel, Hotel 1929 has a good location on Keong Saik Road, is quirky in character, and has rooms from around $150 a night. The rooms are small but cleverly considered, with open-plan bed-and-bathrooms creating more of a studio like space. A great choice for solo travellers, or for couples preferring to spend their travel budget trying out Singapore's food scene (I know I would).

🏠 50 Keong Saik Rd, 089154

🚇 Outram Park or Chinatown

☎ +65 65792026

➹ hotel1929.com

f Hotel 1929

⊙ @hotel1929

$ from $150

Baba House

7 *Peer into the Peranakan Past*

To get a glimpse of yesteryear, book yourself on a tour of the delightful Baba House museum on Neil Road. This bright blue three-story restored townhouse dates back to 1895 and was once the ancestral home of a Peranakan Chinese family. The entrance hall features an impressive ornate altar, with mother-of-pearl inlay chairs and tables positioned around the room. The ancestral hall is stunning, with a breezy air-well for natural cooling and family photos decorating the walls. Upstairs is an elaborate bridal chamber with a gold-gilded Chinese daybed, dressing tables and washbasins. Spot the clever peephole in the floor, which was once used for checking who was knocking at the door. You can visit Baba House by appointment only – email babahouse@nus.edu.sg for their tour schedule.

🏠 157 Neil Rd, 088883

🚌 Outram Park

☎ +65 62275731

↖ nus.edu.sg/museum

f NUS Baba House

$ Free

⊘ By appointment only, email babahouse@nus.edu.sg

Blair Road

8 *Beautiful Heritage Houses*

You know those streets you find in every city where you dream of living. Maybe it's a pastel pink townhouse in a leafy avenue in Notting Hill, London, a tall brownstone building in Brooklyn, New York, or a modern, minimalist home in Nakameguro, Tokyo. For me, the Singapore version has to be Blair Road, a collection of colourful, well preserved 1920s shophouses in the Outram Park area. Lining the road are unique façades painted in baby blues, mint greens and turquoise hues decorated with pretty floral Peranakan tiles. With an interesting mix of Chinese, Malay and European influences, you'll see French-style windows and shutters alongside floral plaster friezes. Originally the homes of wealthy Chinese merchants who moved here in the early 20th century, these mainly private residences are beautifully preserved, with original features. Pick up a coffee from nearby Stranger's Reunion, and spend the morning imaginary house hunting!

Blair Rd, 089955

Outram Park

Tiong Bahru

Quiet Quaint Quarter

With its low-rise buildings defined by art-deco architecture, the Tiong Bahru neighbourhood looks more like Miami than central Singapore. The pre-war housing estate was first built in the 1930s, and is said to have been the area where wealthy Chinese businessmen housed their mistresses.

Tiong Bahru is now a flourishing multicultural community, where old-school charm mixes with the modern. Walking down one street, you'll come across spicy Sichuan and seafood restaurants with live crabs swimming in tanks. Then around the corner, you'll find a road filled with independent bookshops, coffee and cupcake stores and yoga studios. Find a 1920s Monkey God Temple along the same street as a French bakery, and an old kopitiam noodle shop sharing its space with a fancy Japanese yakitori restaurant.

The neighbourhood is anchored by the bustling Tiong Bahru Market, where you can start your day with breakfast in the upstairs hawker centre and then stock up on fresh fish, flowers and fruit from the traditional wet market on the ground floor.

Although the neighbourhood has gone through gentrification over the last few years, its original charm prevails. You will see locals sitting on stalls on the street drinking cups of kopi, men heaving bags of rice and bottles of oyster sauce in and out of the provision shop, or an aunty perched by her living room window, offering a quick shoe-repair service. This is the appeal for me. You may well see me wandering down the leafy alleys, and if you do, please come and say hi!

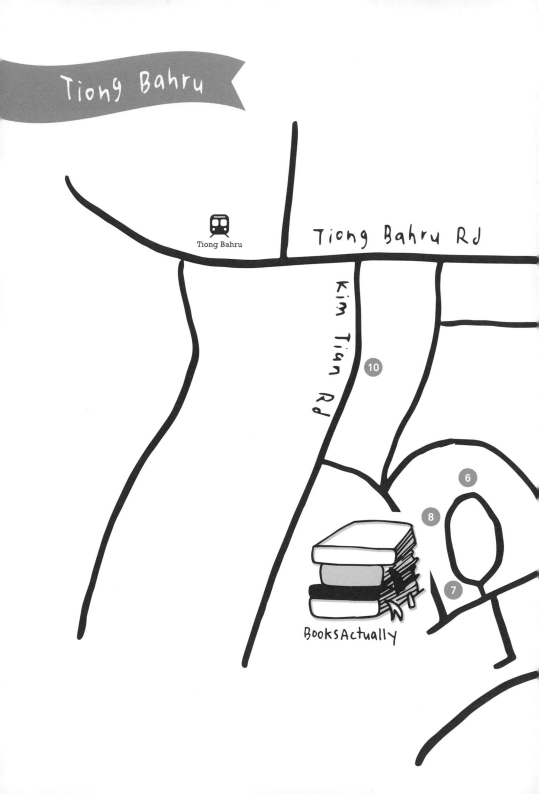

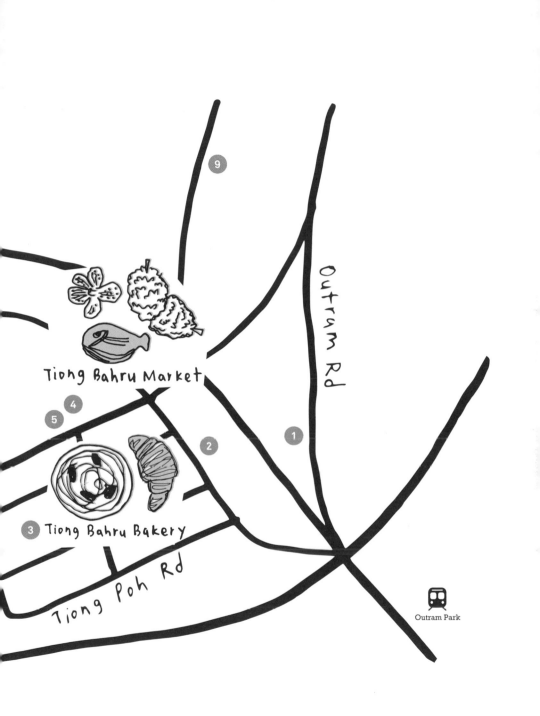

Tiong Bahru Market

Tiong Bahru Bakery

Tiong Poh Rd

Outram Rd

Outram Park

Tiong Bahru Pau

1 *Streetfood-Style Snacks*

Grabbing a selection of snacks from Tiong Bahru Pau has become quite a regular habit of mine, especially since I walk past the store most days to get to the bus stop on Outram Road. A small take-away store, its counters are piled high with stacks of bamboo steamer cases housing the most delightful and delicious dim sum. For a few dollars, pick up a handful of hot BBQ pork buns (char siu bao), and a supply of Cantonese style siu mai. For those with a sweet tooth, they've also got towers of egg tarts. The dim sum here is as fresh as you'll get it, and you can have a peek in the kitchen behind the storefront to see the busy hands at work. In business since 1969, Tiong Bahru Pau have made quite a name for themselves and have also set up shops around the city - look out for their outlets in Tiong Bahru Market, Chinatown, Jurong and Toa Payoh.

🏠 237 Outram Rd, 169041

🚇 Outram Road

☎ +65 62227656

⏲ Tues – Sun 7.30am – 10pm
Closed Mon

Tiong Bahru Bakery

2 *French Croissants and Crafted Coffee*

🏠 56 Eng Hoon St, #01-70, 160056

🚇 Tiong Bahru

↖ tiongbahrubakery.com

📘 Tiong Bahru Bakery

📷 @tiongbahrubakery

🕐 Sun – Thurs 8am – 8pm
Fri – Sat 8am – 10pm

After a morning visit to the busy local market, a great spot to slow down the pace, get your caffeine fix and pause for some pastry goodness is Tiong Bahru Bakery. I'm a pretty big croissant fan, so was over the moon to have stumbled across this place on arrival to the city. The French are one of the biggest expat communities in Singapore and Tiong Bahru, and this may well have played a part in the decision to open a French bakery in this hood. Big crispy croissants come with delicious fruity jams, and addictive sugary kouign-amann and pain au chocolats will tempt you to fall off the detox wagon. For fussy coffee lovers, you've come to the right place. They brew their coffee using freshly ground beans from sister cafe, Common Man Coffee Roasters. Very busy on the weekends; come for breakfast on a weekday to avoid the crowds.

Por Kee Eating House

 *Old-School Chinese Zi Char*

Don't be put off by Por Kee's location in the middle of a car park on Seng Poh Lane. This place does the best Zi Char food — which is essentially affordable, home-style Chinese food meant to be enjoyed with a group of your friends and family. Don't take my word for it; just look at the hundreds of people that pack out this restaurant every evening. Simply pull up a red plastic chair and sit under a tall palm tree — a complete antithesis to the experience you would have in a mall. Be sure to order the champagne-pork ribs, Thai-style steamed fish and cereal-fried prawns. Laid back and authentic with bossy aunties and uncles running the show, Por Kee is not to be missed for an alternative Singapore supper spot.

69 Seng Poh Ln, #01-02, 160069

Tiong Bahru

+65 62210582

Thurs – Tues 11.30-2.30pm
5.30-11.30pm
Closed Wed

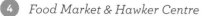

Tiong Bahru Market

4 *Food Market & Hawker Centre*

Life in Tiong Bahru centres around the market, which was established all the way back in 1955. On the ground floor you will find the wet market, with stalls selling bright-pink dragon fruits and ripe yellow Thai mangoes, piles of green bok choy and Japanese cucumber, purple orchids and a variety of palm leaves, as well as fresh salmon and snapper. It's best to come early to this part of the market (I normally turn up at 8am), to ensure a supply of good produce. Upstairs is the hawker centre, a typical Singaporean food court filled with a variety of local cuisines. The rule of thumb is to go to the stall with the longest queue, although this depends on how hungry you are, and how long you mind waiting. I love the char kway teow stall run by an 80-year-old uncle who's been perfecting his trade since his 20s.

🏠 30 Seng Poh Rd, 168898

🚇 Tiong Bahru

➤ tiongbahru.market

🕐 Vary from stall to stall.
The best time to visit is in
the morning.

Loo's Hainanese Curry Rice

5 *Superb Street Food*

When walking around Tiong Bahru looking for Loo's Hainanese Curry Rice, the easiest indicator is to spot the line of people patiently queuing on Seng Poh Road, waiting to get a taste of this famous curry. Loo's is always busy, whether it's around breakfast or lunch (it's not open for dinner), but the queue moves quickly. Sometimes on a Sunday, my boyfriend will give me a knowing glance and say – *'fancy Loo's for lunch?'*. Yes, it's become a habit. The main event is the fried pork chop, with sides of cabbage stew, aubergine and fluffy rice topped with a fried egg, which I like to have with a cold, refreshing oolong tea. This food stall has simple seating, with plastic stools and small tables perched on the pavement. Remember to bring your own tissues as eating here can get messy (most street food places don't provide them).

🏠 71 Seng Poh Rd #01-49, 160071

🚇 Tiong Bahru

⏱ Mon – Sun 8am – 2.30pm

Bincho

6 *Hidden Japanese Gem*

People passing by the 70-year-old traditional kopitiam coffee shop on Moh Guan Terrace should have no reason to believe it is anything other than that. But lo and behold, when you step into the back entrance of Hua Bee you enter into Bincho – a whole Harry Potter platform 9 and ¾-esque world where simple bak chore mee is replaced by a yakitori filled Osaka wonderland. Choose between the set 11-course menu, or pick and mix from the a la carte menu displayed on the wall. I like the scallop sashimi, grilled asparagus, wagyu beef and charcoaled chicken. This is probably one of my top spots in Singapore, not just for the food, but for the 'back door' atmosphere and the attention to detail, such as the old marble tables, quirky chopstick holders and mix and match sake cups.

78 Moh Guan Ter, #01-19, 162078

Tiong Bahru

+65 64384567

bincho.com.sg

Bincho at Hua Bee

@binchosg

Tues – Sun. 12pm-3pm. 6pm-12am
Closed Mon

Plain Vanilla Bakery

 7 *Cupcakes & Coffee*

🏠 1D Yong Siak St, 168641

🚇 Tiong Bahru

☎ +65 83637614

🡥 plainvanillabakery.com

📘 Plain Vanilla Bakery

⏱ Mon – Sat 8am – 7pm
Sun 9am – 6pm

Arguably the best cupcake shop in Singapore, Plain Vanilla wins for both taste and design. Wander past the blue Dutch bicycles and wooden swing outside the cafe, and into the bakery where all the magic happens. Fresh cakes are made in front of your eyes using what they describe as the best of ingredients: 'French butter, pure Madagascar Bourbon vanilla, bittersweet Belgian chocolate'. My favourites are the Earl Grey and the Strawberry and White chocolate flavours. I must admit that I visit this place more often than is healthy! They also deliver if you need a great last minute birthday/ house warming/get well soon present. They do scrumptious grilled sandwiches and salads for lunch, and on weekends they have a brunch menu that includes baked eggs on brioche with mixed berries.

BooksActually

8 *Beautiful Books & Local Literature*

In this wonderful independent bookshop on Yong Siak Street, Kenny Leck and his team have carefully curated a range of beautiful books by local writers and artists as well as much loved titles from international authors. On the shelves you will find poetry, short stories and novels alongside quirky cookbooks and photography books. Strong supporters of the local literature scene, under their own imprint, *Math Paper Press*, they publish works from up-and-coming and established Singaporean writers and poets, and often hold in-store author conversations for their loyal community. The BooksActually 'elves' as they call themselves are very knowledgeable and helpful for when you're wondering what next to read. The shop is also a great place to pick up hard-to-find indie magazines, as well as fresh titles from local niche zines.

🏠 9 Yong Siak St, 168645

🚍 Tiong Bahru

☎ +65 62229195

🔝 booksactuallyshop.com

✉ shop@booksactually.com

📘 BooksActually

📷 @booksactually

🕐 Sun – Mon 10am – 6pm
Tues – Sat 10am – 8pm

Tan Boon Liat Building

9 *Unique Homewares & Furniture Finds*

This old industrial building on Outram Road looks like the last place you would expect to find homeware gems, but it just so happens to be pretty fab, if Asian antiques are your thing. Start on the ground floor and check out **Red House**, which sells ornate Chinese cabinets, console tables and huge carved mirrors, and **Fairprice** which sells turquoise console tables, traditional medicine cabinets and smaller home accessories. On the seventh floor you'll find **Singapore Trading Post**, which stocks colonial-inspired home décor objects like palm-covered cushions and vintage travel posters. My favourite shop of them all though is **Artful House** on the eighth floor. They have beautiful console tables made from old carved-wooden doors and window frames found in Rajasthan in India, and side tables that were formerly intricately made dowry chests.

315 Outram Rd, #08-04
Tan Boon Liat Building, 169074

Tiong Bahru

Vary from shop to shop

Grey Projects

10 *Secret Artists' Space*

I must have walked past the entrance to Grey Projects a dozens times, and never knew it existed. It took my friend Audrey (owner of Yeo Workshop in Gillman Barracks) to show me this awesome, albeit hidden, contemporary art gallery on the third floor of a residential apartment block. Run by artists for artists, Grey Projects puts on regular exhibitions of works by members of the local art scene. It also hosts international collaborations through its on-site artist-in-residency program bringing in talent from places such as Bandung, Taipei, Barcelona and Columbia. Importantly, Grey Projects works to fill the gap in the Singapore art scene by holding challenging shows that wouldn't normally appear in bigger galleries. Past shows include installations by gay artists with a LGBTQ theme, and works exploring the migrant labour issues in the city. Check their Facebook page for regular artists talks and new exhibitions.

🏠 6B Kim Tian Rd, 169246 (next to 7/11)

🚇 Tiong Bahru

☎ +65 6655 6492

🔍 greyprojects.org

📘 Grey Projects

💲 Free

🕐 Wed – Fri 1pm – 7pm
Sat 1pm – 6pm
Closed Sun – Tues

Orchard & River Valley

Shopping Mecca & Riverside Region

Once a small avenue leading to fruit trees, nutmeg plantations and pepper farms, Orchard Road has since swapped its spices for shops and is now a hub for international designer stores and a seemingly endless supply of deep cavernous malls. Entrepreneur Tang Choon Keng was a pioneer in the development of this stretch, establishing his namesake high-end shopping mall Tangs in 1958. The Orchard area is now home to big name brands from all over the world, as well as specialty shops catering to the prosperous Asian shoppers.

South of the bustling street, towards the Singapore River, is the River Valley area, a favourite stomping ground for expats who have set up their home in the city. A few large warehouse buildings still line the waterside, a reminder of the days when this was an important trade route. These have now been converted into lofty cafes, wine bars and restaurants serving the cosmopolitan community.

Fort Canning Park provides a breath of fresh air, nestled within these otherwise busy, developed neighbourhoods. The park is lovely for a leisurely stroll or cool early morning jog under the towering ancient trees.

When you reach the river, hop on a boat to take you up to Marina Bay, giving you a quick tour of Clarke Quay and Boat Quay on your way.

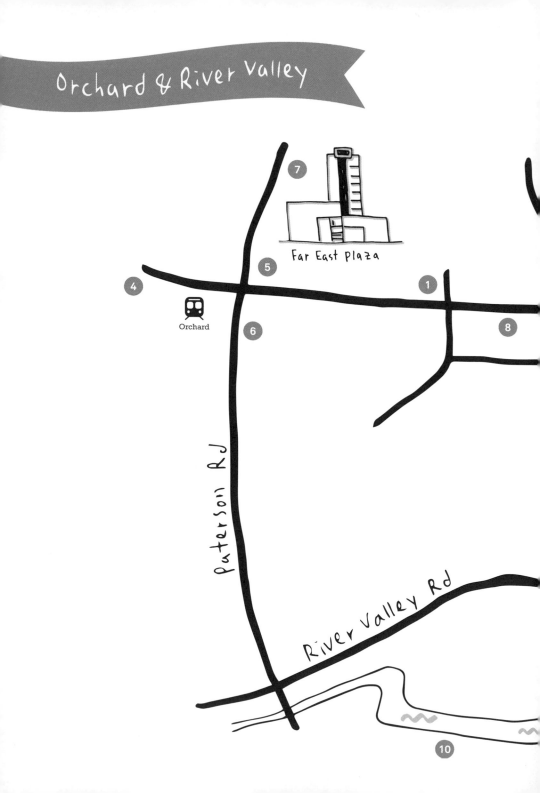

Orchard & River Valley

Far East Plaza

Orchard

Paterson Rd

River Valley Rd

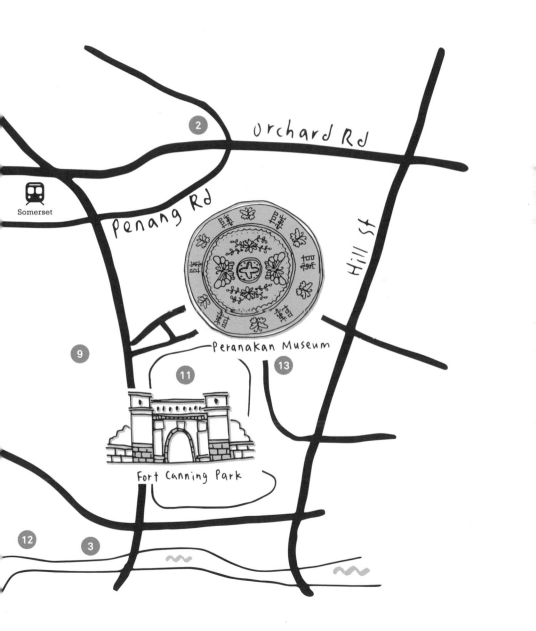

Orchard Rd

Penang Rd

Somerset

Hill St

Peranakan Museum

Fort Canning Park

Imperial Treasure Super Peking Duck

1 *Delicious Duck*

🏠 #05-42/45 Paragon,
290 Orchard Rd, 238859

🚇 Orchard

☎ +65 67327838

↖ imperialtreasure.com

📘 Imperial Treasure

🕐 Mon – Sun 11.30am – 2.45pm,
6pm – 10.30pm

My weekends in Singapore often end with a comforting Sunday afternoon meal, a vague attempt to recreate that roast dinner tradition that we have back in the UK. Although I wouldn't normally suggest eating in a shiny shopping mall, Imperial Treasure Super Peking Duck in Paragon is an exception. Call up a couple of days in advance to order a whole Peking duck (or two) which will be served roasted to perfection, using centuries-old methods from the Emperor's imperial kitchen in Beijing. Once you're seated, the skilled chefs carefully carve up the crispy duck into slices, ready to be hand wrapped into thin pancakes, with dollops of hoisin sauce – delish! A visit to Imperial Treasure feels truly and authentically Chinese, and is a great way to sample the flavours of Beijing in Southeast Asia. I definitely recommend it for a group, family-style Sunday supper.

Tomi Sushi

② *Sublime Japanese Seafood*

Singapore has plenty of sushi spots, catering to the demands of thousands of Japanese expats with exacting standards, and Tomi Sushi was recommended to me by one such reliable source. Although the food centre where it is located looks quite commercial, when you step inside the small and unassuming Tomi Sushi, you'll find a tiny taste of Japan. I recommend sitting inside (not on the hot, noisy terrace outside), and if possible at the counter seats where you've got the perfect view of the performance of sushi making by the talented chefs. Originating from the Niigata prefecture in Japan , where it first opened its doors in 1954, Tomi Sushi is particular about its produce, using only 100% Koshihikari rice from its hometown, Japanese sea salt, traditionally brewed soy sauce and live seafood imported directly from Japan. Ask the chef to serve up what has come fresh that day – I'm a tuna addict and could happily plough through different cuts of this fish - otoro, chutoro and akami – all placed carefully on thick tender rice.

🏠 35 Cuppage Rd, Cuppage Terrace, 229459

🚇 Somerset

☎ +65 63334633

🔖 tomisushi.asia

📘 Tomi Sushi

🕐 Mon – Sun 5pm – 12am

Robertson Quay

3 *Riverside Neighbourhood*

Robertson Quay is a relaxed residential neighbourhood by the river popular with expats. Although not the most Singaporean of locations, it has some great food spots. Here are a few favourites for brunch and dinner:

Common Man Coffee Roasters

Taking its cue from the esteemed Australian coffee culture, Common Man serves some of the best of the black stuff in Singapore. The food is fabulous too – I highly recommend the 'Turkish Common Man Breakfast' with gooey phyllo-wrapped soft-boiled egg, balls of squidgy fried feta with hummus and pita bread.

🏠 22 Martin Rd, #01-00, 239058

↖ commonmancoffeeroasters.com

⊘ Mon – Sun 7.30am – 6pm

Super Loco

Sister of the marvellous Mexican restaurant Lucha Loco, Super Loco is a brilliant brunch spot by the river. I like to come here for a Saturday morning açai super bowl fruit fix followed by the super huevos rancheros with black beans and a dollop of guac. The refreshing 'sans alcohol' cocktails are a handy hangover cure. FYI brunch is only on weekends.

🏠 The Quayside, 60 Robertson Quay, #01-13, 238252

↖ super-loco.com

⊘ Mon – Fri: 5pm – 12am
Sat – Sun: 10am – 12am

Yakiniku Yazawa

After a trip to Tokyo, I decided that Japanese BBQ is a strong contender for one of the world's best meals. Yazawa is a top-notch BBQ joint serving the finest selection of kuroge wagyu, that expert chefs cook in front of you on a grill built into your table. Note, the high quality of the meat means that the bill can be pretty pricey!

🏠 11 Unity St #01-01
Robertson Walk, 237995

⤢ yazawameat.com

☎ +65 62352941

⊘ Mon – Sun 6pm – 11.30pm

Sushi Kaishin

A small and intimate sushi spot tucked away down a side alley, Sushi Kaishin is a 12-seater counter restaurant frequented mainly by Japanese (always a good sign). Go for the omakase menu (meaning 'I'll leave it up to you'), where the chef will prepare portions of hirame, ika, ikura and otoro sushi to name a few.

🏠 30 Robertson Quay, #01-04,
Riverside View, 238251

☎ +65 67333720

⊘ Mon – Sat 11.30 – 3pm, 6pm – 11pm
Closed Sun

Edit Lifestyle

4 *Bohemian Resort Shop*

Shops along Orchard Road selling independent, design focused finds are few and far between, so thank goodness for the gorgeous Edit Lifestyle! The light-filled boutique is like a summer holiday in a shop. Glamorous swimwear and floaty beaded kaftans line the rails, with straw hats and cool sunglasses on the shelves. It's filled with objects sourced from the owner's travels around the world, so you're likely to spot pieces crafted by artisans from Uzbekistan, or trinkets found in Turkish bazaars. Splash out on fine art photography displayed on the walls, or give yourself a small treat with a coffee table book. Great for gifts, Edit Lifestyle regularly refreshes its offerings, with new finds added every couple of months.

137-139 Tanglin Rd,
Tudor Court, 247927

Orchard Road

+65 68365686

editlifestyle.com

boutique@editlifestyle.com

edit lifestyle

Mon – Sat 10am – 7pm
Sun 10am – 5pm

Tangs

5 *Locally-led Department Store*

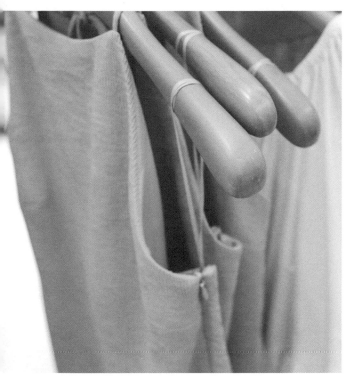

On first impressions, Tangs looks like any other department store, as you walk past counter tops weighed down with global makeup and beauty brands. Go upstairs though and you'll be delighted with the fashion and homewear labels here. You see, in Singapore, it's almost impossible for local brands to have a physical presence (due to sky-high rents), but luckily Tangs supports smaller Singaporean brands that might otherwise not have a platform. Tangs also partners with the local college of the arts, LASALLE, with their buyers working closely with the fashion students to develop collections that are then sold in the store, how cool! Other local brands on sale here include the contemporary and affordable Collate, feminine and lacey Aijek, religo-pop label Amenpapa from Hong Kong and pretty pleated dresses from Chinese designer Bysm. The fourth floor houses lifestyle and homeware brands, with intricate ikat bags and cushions, deliciously scented candles and also a Bynd Artisan stand for personalised notebooks and paper accessories.

🏠 310 Orchard Rd, 238864

🚇 Orchard

📞 +65 67375500

↖ tangs.com

f Tangs

📷 @tangssg

⊘ Mon – Sat 10.30am – 9.30pm
Sun 11am – 8.30pm

In Good Company

6 *Singapore Silhouettes*

It took me a while to find local brands that are affordable, accessible, stylish, and doing something a little bit different. I've been a big fan of the young start-up label In Good Company ever since spotting their pieces at Tangs, and they now have their own flagship store in ION. Their clothes have been designed with the tropical climate in mind, and are fun and full of colour as well as feeling modern and minimalistic. Going beyond the treadmill of trends and seasons (as there are none in Singapore!), IGC sells soft structured pastel hued tops, floaty white shirts, burnt orange t-shirts with tie-ups, as well as stocking their own chunky statement tribal-esque jewellery. With the addition of sweet treats from my favourite supplier, Plain Vanilla, alongside piles of indie magazines, IGC feels more like a cool concept store, where you can meet a friend for a coffee, have a bite to eat and then pick out an outfit for Friday night.

🏠 ION Orchard #B1-06, 2 Orchard Turn, 238801

🚇 Orchard

🔗 ingoodcompany.asia

📘 In Good Company

📷 @igcasia

🕐 Mon – Sun 10.30am – 9.30pm

Far East Plaza

7 *One-Stop Shop*

I have many a friend who is totally obsessed with Far East Plaza - a one-stop shop for everything you did and didn't know you needed. It might look tired and run down compared to the newer, luxurious Orchard malls, but Far East Plaza houses all the gems and here are a few of my favourites:

Mohan's Custom Tailors (#02-73): bring in a photo of what you'd like made, and they'll create a carbon copy. Done. I love my cobalt blue silk kimono, which is the most luxurious piece of loungewear. It's also great for guys looking for smart suits and stylish shirts.

The Sushi Bar (#04-28): you're going to need some sustenance after you've shopped 'til you've dropped. Affordable, quick and tasty – go for the chirashi don sashimi bowls.

D'Sire Hair (#02-08): if you need your locks chopped, head to the guys at D'Sire Hair, who will work their magic and leave you with change for $50.

🏠 14 Scotts Rd, Singapore 228213

🚇 Orchard

↖ fareastplaza.com.sg

⊘ Mon – Sun 10.00am – 10.00pm

Choo Yilin

8 *Gorgeous Jade Jewellery*

🏠 Mandarin Gallery #02-23, 333A Orchard Rd, 238897

🚉 Somerset MRT

☎ +65 67331131

🏹 chooyilin.com

📘 Choo Yilin – Fine Jeweller

📷 @chooyilin

🕑 Mon – Sun 11.00am – 9.00pm

If you're looking for an authentic but contemporary Southeast Asian souvenir, I suggest you pop into this jewellery store founded by Singaporean Choo Yilin. The brand began as a social enterprise working with the hill tribe artisans in northern Thailand. Working mainly with Type A Burmese jadeite, Choo Yilin takes the traditional and locally revered stone, and gives it a modern twist, while using motifs that nod to Asian culture. Reflecting icons such as bamboo shoots, sakaru flowers and Peranakan kebaya dress, the designs are cool, classic and a fresh take on the plain jade bangles that have traditionally been worn as protection from harm. Choo Yilin has become a local hit for Si Dian Jin, a four-piece set of wedding jewellery given to the bride by the groom's mother in the Chinese tradition. The perfect place to pick up a gift to remind you of your time here in Singapore; I've got my eye on one of the bamboo pieces for my next birthday.

Lloyd's Inn

9 *Tranquil Tropical Hideaway*

It's hard to believe that you can find a quiet, trendy, contemporary design hotel just a stone's throw away from busy Orchard Road for an affordable price — oh, and all rooms at Lloyd's Inn come with breezy outdoor showers, and there's a refreshing dipping pool in the garden too. The aesthetic of the hotel reflects Scandinavian and Japanese minimalism with lots of cool concrete, clean lines and uncluttered rooms, as well as lush greenery giving guests that Balinese feel. The hotel has 34 rooms, ranging from garden rooms with private outdoor areas, to the sky rooms with outdoor bathtubs, where you can bathe under twinkling stars at night. I really like the outdoor area, where you can lounge around on daybeds or hang out in suspended wicker chairs, while also getting some relief from the sticky Singapore weather by taking a dip in the pool. Note, there is no restaurant or cafe on site, so head to nearby Killiney Road and try Real Food for ethically sourced, homemade meals.

🏠 2 Lloyd Rd, 239091

🚌 Somerset

☎ +65 67377309

🔍 lloydsinn.com

✉ mail@lloydsinn.com

f Lloyd's Inn

⊙ @lloydsinn

$ From $180

The Warehouse Hotel

10 *Stylish Riverside Retreat*

Built in 1895, this space began its life as a 'godown' (warehouse) during Singapore's days in the spice trade. Then in the 1980s, it was converted to a disco joint welcoming throngs of partygoers. Today it has been revived as an intimate, 37-room boutique hotel, catering to those who like a punch of personality alongside their pillows. Spread over two floors, the hotel feels spacious, and has everything you need for a sophisticated city break. The restaurant, Po, is not only designed like a dream, but created in collaboration with the wonderful chef Willin Low, of Wild Rocket fame, serving up modern dishes as well as Singaporean classics. The double height lobby is a happening hangout, with comfy banquette seating, and a cool corner bar serving drinks inspired by the building's vibrant past. Book yourself a river-view room, tuck into the mini bar with locally-sourced snacks and spot other cool collaborations such as bed spreads from Singaporean label Matter and mugs from Mud Rock Ceramics.

🏠 320 Havelock Rd, 169628

🚉 Outram Park

☎ +65 68280000

↖ thewarehousehotel.com

✉ reservations@thewarehousehotel.com

f The Warehouse Hotel

⊙ @thewarehousehotel

Ⓢ From $285

Fort Canning Park

11 *City Centre Escape*

Located in the heart of the city centre, Fort Canning Park is a tranquil respite to Singapore's concrete jungle and a leafy slice of yesteryear. Once home to the palaces of 14th century Malay Kings, this is also the site where Sir Stamford Raffles built his bungalow in the 19th century. Now the hilltop park is a shady spot for an evening stroll where you can walk through the Fort Gate (a remnant of the fortress built here), and enjoy the aromas of nutmeg and clove from the spice garden while admiring the huge heritage trees towering above. Fort Canning Park also plays host to beautifully curated events, such as outdoor theatre and ballet performances and cinema shows under the stars. For a fancy lunch in an old black and white bungalow, book a table at the lovely Lewin Terrace, which serves fabulous Japanese food.

River Valley Rd, 179037

 Clarke Quay

Singapore Tyler Print Institute

12 *Paper-Focused Platform*

The STPI is an internationally renowned gallery and workshop space dedicated to innovative print and papermaking techniques. With its location on the main stretch of Robertson Quay, it's a place that more people should really know about. At the core of the institute is the six to eight week residency programme for leading artists from around the world – past artists include British-Iranian Shirazeh Houshiary, Shinro Ohtake from Japan, Jane Lee from Singapore and Heri Dono from Indonesia. They collaborate with the in-house team in the fields of relief printing, lithography, etching, screen printing and papermaking, often working with methods unfamiliar to their normal mediums. Come for their guided tours (Tues and Thurs at 11.30am and Sat at 2pm) and look out for artists' talks and workshops throughout the year.

🏠 41 Robertson Quay, 238236

🚇 Clarke Quay

☎ +65 63363663

↖ stpi.com.sg

✉ stpi@stpi.com.sg

f STPI – Creative Workshop & Gallery

⊙ @stpi_gallery

$ Free

⊘ Mon – Fri 10am – 7pm
Sat 9am – 6pm
Closed Sun and PH

Peranakan Museum

13 *People of Singapore's Past*

🏠 39 Armenian St, 179941

🚏 City Hall or Bras Basah

➤ peranakanmuseum.org.sg

📘 Peranakan Museum Singapore

📷 @peranakanmuseum

💲 $10

🕐 Sat-Thurs 10am – 7pm
Fri 10am – 9pm

During your time in Singapore you'll hear many references to the Peranakan people and their culture. The word Peranakan means 'child', or 'born of' in Malay, and refers to the community of descendants of travelling traders who stayed to marry local women. The best way to understand more about this particular community and their culture is to visit the fascinating Peranakan Museum, housed in the former Tao Nan Chinese School, just by Fort Canning Park. Explore rooms with artifacts from traditional Peranakan weddings, including examples of Nyonya needlework on items such as beautiful beaded slippers stitched with thousands of tiny colourful beads, and exquisite examples of wedding porcelain painted with butterflies. Admire the Peranakan fashion such as pretty patterned kebayas with embellished blouses, bright skirts and layers of lovely jewellery. Don't miss the stunning beadwork tablecloth. Created in Penang in the early 20th century for a twelve-day wedding ceremony, it has over a million glass beads and is one of the largest and most important pieces of Peranakan beadwork in existence.

Dempsey Hill & Bukit Timah

Lush, Verdant City Spaces

Singapore is fondly known as the Garden City, and as you start venturing beyond Orchard Road towards the northwest, you'll soon see why. The stunning Botanic Gardens are a stone's throw away from the busy shopping streets, providing much needed breathing space for the city's inhabitants and visitors. Take shade under the old Tembusu trees or the wide Kapok trees and wander through the Cool House in the National Orchid Garden, the tropical highland cloud forest, which is home to spectacular blooms such as those native to Sulawesi and Borneo.

South of the Botanic Gardens is Dempsey Hill. Formerly an army barracks, the heritage buildings provide breezy spaces for relaxing restaurants, antique shops and art galleries, with the additional advantage of lovely lush greenery surrounding the area. Spend a lazy weekend here enjoying a long lunch with friends.

North of the Botanic Gardens is Bukit Timah, where the landscape starts to get more wild and unruly. Beyond roads of residential homes there are parks and nature reserves that make the area feel delightfully less urban. As you approach the green expanse of MacRitchie Park, surrounding a cool blue reservoir, you might see monkeys swinging from tree to tree and diverse examples of wildlife hidden in the thick flora.

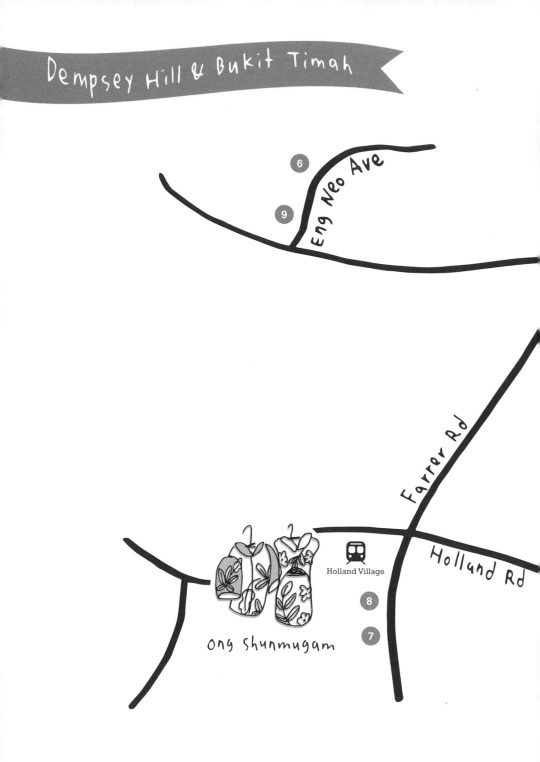

Dempsey Hill & Bukit Timah

6

Eng Neo Ave

9

Farrer Rd

Holland Village

Holland Rd

8

7

Ong Shunmugam

Bukit Timah Rd

Botanic Gardens

Cluny Rd

Singapore
Botanic Gardens

Open Farm Community

Open Farm Community

① *Leafy Lunchtime Locale*

A wonderful escape from the city, Open Farm Community is a lovely restaurant set in a garden amongst the lush greenery of Dempsey Hill. See tropical flowers bursting alongside gorgeous sculptures and mango trees, and try your hand at playing boules on the lawn. I love the whole ethos behind the restaurant, which sets out to 'connect the community to nature and celebrate local spirit'. They've teamed up with Edible Garden City, a social enterprise that champions the idea of growing food in under-utilised spaces like rooftops and sidewalks. Brunch here is the best – make sure you order the buttermilk pancakes with açai berries and homemade granola, and I also love the mud-crab pappardelle with Thai curry sauce, squash and coconut. OFC is a perfect place for a long Saturday session with some pals, with tables full of pasta, accompanied by glasses of pale rosé.

🏠 130E Minden Rd, 248819

🚃 Orchard (30 mins walk away)

☎ +65 64710306

↖ openfarmcommunity.com

📘 Open Farm Community

📷 @openfarmcommunity

🕐 Mon – Fri 12pm – 4pm, 6pm – 10pm
Sat – Sun 11am – 4pm, 6pm – 10pm

Morsels

2 *Hidden Fusion Hangout*

The lovely chef and owner Petrina Loh used to live in San Francisco, and she's created a laid-back California meets Singapore vibe infused in both the food and the atmosphere at Morsels. She likes to blend different techniques with Asian flavours from Japan, Korea, Thailand etc, with a nod to trends from the American west coast. Start with small plates such as Asian greens and burrata salad, Hokkaido scallop ceviche and tom kha leche de tigre. Petrina takes a lot of time and care to find suppliers, so you'll be having the best grilled wild Sri Lankan tiger prawns, and the most stunning smoked strawberry gazpacho. My favourite dish of them all is the steamed venus clams with California figs, fig broth, homemade kimchi and pickled Japanese seaweed. Morsels is a must for a casual midweek dinner in the Dempsey area.

🏠 25 Dempsey Rd, 249670

🚇 Holland Village (25 mins walk away)

☎ +65 62663822

🖱 morsels.com.sg

✉ reservations@morsels.com.sg

📘 Morsels

📷 @morselsinsingapore

🕑 Tues – Fri 12pm – 3pm, 6pm-11pm
Sat 10.30am – 3pm, 6pm-11pm
Closed Sun – Mon

Chopsuey Cafe

3 *Nostalgic & Chic Chinese*

🏠 Block 10, Dempsey Rd,
#01-23, 247700

🚇 Orchard (30 mins walk away)

☎ +65 92246611

🖋 pscafe.com/chopsuey-cafe-at-
dempsey-hill

📘 Chopsuey Cafe

📷 @chopsueycafe

🕐 Mon – Fri 11.30am – 11pm
Sat – Sun 10.30am – 11pm

Located in a charming black and white bungalow in Dempsey Hill looking over a stretch of lush green jungle, Chopsuey gives you a feel for old-school Singapore with a contemporary twist. Jazz music plays softly in the background as you are served steamed dim sum baskets on marble-top tables. They've taken inspiration from food tasted in Chinese restaurants in the Western world – an Anglicised concept that differs from the traditional Chinese restaurants in Singapore. I always order the crispy duck pow pockets, san choy pau (minced pork and chicken in lettuce cups), tingling chilli jam prawns with Szechuan peppercorns, and chopsuey chopsuey - garlicy wok fried veggies. Grab a cocktail before dinner – I like the Lily's lychee martini with chilli infused vodka.

Blu Kouzina

4 *Great Greek Eats*

When you've had enough plates of char kway teow and over ordered on dim sum dumplings, you could be tempted to mix up your diet with some Mediterranean food, with there being no better place to find it that the brilliant Greek restaurant Blu Kouzina. Step inside a light filled, whitewashed taverna with splashes of bright blue. Book a table in the airy conservatory room at the back, with large windows giving you a view over the green cricket ground. A great venue for groups or parties, its food is definitely designed for sharing, with marvellous mezes such as tzatziki, taramasalata, and melitzanosalata (smoked eggplant salad). Feast on grilled lamb chops, squid and seabass, alongside moussaka and a traditional Greek salad. Get me to the Greek!

🏠 Block 10, Dempsey Rd, #01-21, 247700

🚐 Orchard (30 mins walk away)

☎ +65 68750872

↖ blukouzina.com/SG

f Blu Kouzina

🕐 Mon – Thurs 6pm-10pm
Fri – Sun 12am – 2.30pm, 6pm – 10pm

Corner House

 Gastronomy in a Garden

🏠 E.J.H. Corner House, 1 Cluny Rd, Nassim Gate, Singapore Botanic Gardens, 259569

🚇 Botanic Gardens

☎ +65 64691000

↖ cornerhouse.com.sg

f Corner House – Singapore Botanic Gardens

📷 @cornerhousesg

⊘ Tues – Sat 12pm – 3pm, 6.30pm – 11pm
Sun 11.30am – 3pm, 6.30pm – 11pm
Closed Mon

If you're looking for a really romantic restaurant in a stunning setting, with world class Singaporean food, then look no further than Corner House, set discreetly amongst the lush foliage in the Botanic Gardens. The building holds a lovely story - being the former home of E.J.H. Corner, a British botanist who taught coconut-picking monkeys to gather botanical samples. The chef at the helm is Jason Tan, a young Singaporean, who, using his classical French training, has created a new contemporary cuisine concept 'Gastro Botanica'. He heroes the simplest of ingredients, such as the 'variation of best seasonal tomatoes', prepared using the following methods: natural, marinated, confit, sorbet, cloud and vintage sherry. He uses onion for his signature dish. Chef Jason used to hate onions, but now champions the root, creating a unique onion tea infused with earl grey. For dessert, try the local dishes with a twist, such as the guava sorbet, kaya toast or salted egg custard macaroons.

Rider's Cafe

6 *Ride 'n Dine*

I love this little corner of Singapore, where things appear to have been left carefully as they have always been. Rider's Cafe looks over a working riding school, the Bukit Timah Saddle Club, with the most beautiful horses grazing in the fields in front of you. This open-air black and white bungalow is beyond charming, and a brilliant place for brunch. After getting a round of Bloody Marys in, order the smoked salmon and sweetcorn hash with avocado salsa or treat yourself to the French toast with burnt banana, bacon and honeycomb butter. A romantic retreat, as well as being great for groups, Rider's Cafe is a special spot for those that love a bit of outdoors in the city. It's also a five-minute walk to antique utopia Junkie's Corner down the road.

🏠 51 Fairways Dr, 286965

🚇 Sixth Avenue

☎ +65 64669819

🔺 riderscafe.sg

📘 Riders Cafe

📷 @riderscafe

🕐 Sun – Thurs 8am – 9pm
Fri – Sat 8am – 10pm
Closed Mon

Ong Shunmugam

7 *Fantastic Asian Fashion*

Founded by the incredibly inspiring Priscilla Shunmugam, *(read her interview on p169)*, Ong Shunmugam is one of the most brilliant fashion brands in Singapore. Priscilla began her career in the law, which led her to create a brand with a strong analytical approach with deep thinking about her cultural creations. Located on the Jalan Merah Saga stretch in Holland Village, the beautifully designed showroom also houses a busy on-site atelier, where you can see rolls of exquisite textiles being sewn together through a glass screen at the back of the store. Shop for stylish floral cheongsam dresses with mandarin collars in silk brocade, wrap dresses with Japanese obi belts and lace embroidered skirts in pretty pale hues. As well as the ready-to-wear collections the brand does custom productions such as eveningwear or bridal designs, reinterpreted with a contemporary angle on Southeast Asian influences such as Chinese, Indian, Malay, Peranakan and Sikh styles.

🏠 43 Jalan Merah Saga, #01-76, 278115

🚇 Holland Village

☎ +65 62522612

↖ ongshunmugam.com

📘 Ong Shunmugam

📷 @ongshunmugam

🕐 Mon – Sun 12pm - 7pm

Bynd Artisan

8 *Beautiful Personalised Books*

In this digital world that we live in, there's no better treat than having your own personalised book made for you by hand, using traditional typesetting and machinery. The founder of Bynd Artisan, Winnie Chan, was born into a family of bookbinders in Singapore. In tribute to the craftsmen of yesteryear, Bynd Artisan has its own small in-house team who will, in around 20 minutes, create a customised notebook for you. Mix and match from a rainbow of colourful covers, varying spirals and funky fasteners. They then use foil stamping to print your desired lettering on the front (I have a bright-blue notebook with Lost Guides embossed on the cover!). This special store also holds regular workshops in botanical painting, calligraphy and even medieval bookbinding techniques.

🏠 44 Jalan Merah Saga #01-54, 278116

🚇 Holland Village

↖ byndartisan.com

📘 Bynd Artisan

📷 @byndartisan

🕐 Mon – Fri 12pm – 9pm
Sat – Sun 10am – 9pm

Junkie's Corner

9 *Asian Antique Warehouse*

Junkie's Corner is located down an overgrown track near the Turf Club in a huge, albeit tired-looking warehouse. An Aladdin's cave of Asian collectables, it is THE place for well-priced vintage and antique furniture and homewares. You could say that I'm a Junkie's Corner junky - I've spent way too many a weekend meandering down the musty, dusty corridors and sifting through the stacks of shelves to find those tired treasures that need a bit of tlc. Find anything and everything, from oriental painted screens to porcelain elephants to Triumph typewriters. Bigger items include gorgeous marble kopitiam tables in the style of those found in Singapore coffee shops in the 1950s, or Indonesian carved wooden mirrors. For suitcase sized items pick up colourful Chinese vases or miniature tea sets. Allow at least an hour to comb through the layers of wooden console tables, 1970s jukeboxes and apothecary cabinets. Bring cash and prepare to haggle hard with the owners.

🏠 2 Turf Club Rd, 287988

🚇 Sixth Avenue

🕐 Mon – Sun 10.30am – 6pm

Singapore Botanic Gardens

10 *Glorious Tropical Gardens*

A trip to Singapore isn't complete without spending a morning wandering around the beautiful Botanic Gardens. Steeped in over 150 years of history, the 82-hectare garden has been named the first tropical botanical gardens on the UNESCO World Heritage list. Importantly, in the 19th century, rubber seedlings were introduced from Kew Gardens in London and experimented with in Singapore, bringing a prosperous rubber trade to Southeast Asia. Nowadays, visitors can admire spaces like the 'Healing Garden' discovering the invigorating power of plants, alongside the perfume filled 'Fragrant Garden'. Be sure to visit the gorgeous 'National Orchid Garden' with over 1,000 species on display. Look out for the performances that are held outdoors at the stunning symphony lake - from jazz bands to symphony orchestras. For food, there's the lovely Halia or the charming Corner House for special occasions.

🏠 1 Cluny Rd, 259569

🚇 Botanic Gardens

☎ +65 64717138

🖱 sbg.org.sg

📘 Singapore Botanic Gardens

🕐 5am – 12am

💲 Free
$5 for National Orchid Garden

Central & Marina Bay

Modern City Centre

Telok Ayer Street was once the shoreline where migrants landed when they reached Singapore, which is why it is the location of the sea temple, Thian Hock Keng. In the 1970s, land reclamation work began in order to create what we now see as the Marina Bay area, extending the city out to the east. This landscape now appears as the modern Singapore scene; the bright lights of downtown beaming onto the placid bay as the sun begins to set. The centre piece is the iconic Marina Bay Sands building which towers over the city with its ship-shaped top floor, now a beacon for what is considered one of the world's most forward-looking of cities. Behind the bullish buildings lies a horticultural oasis, Gardens by The Bay, with Supertree structures, lush tropical landscaped gardens and clever conservatories providing much-needed respite from the dense development of the city centre.

Head up the river to Boat Quay, the city's commercial centre during its early trading years, when barges would transport goods to be held at the warehouses in Clarke Quay. The quays are now lined with rows of bars, jostling for the passing trade of tourists. North of the river, clusters of museums and art galleries housed in heritage buildings are gaining momentum on the international scene, holding a rotation of exciting exhibitions with a unique Asian perspective.

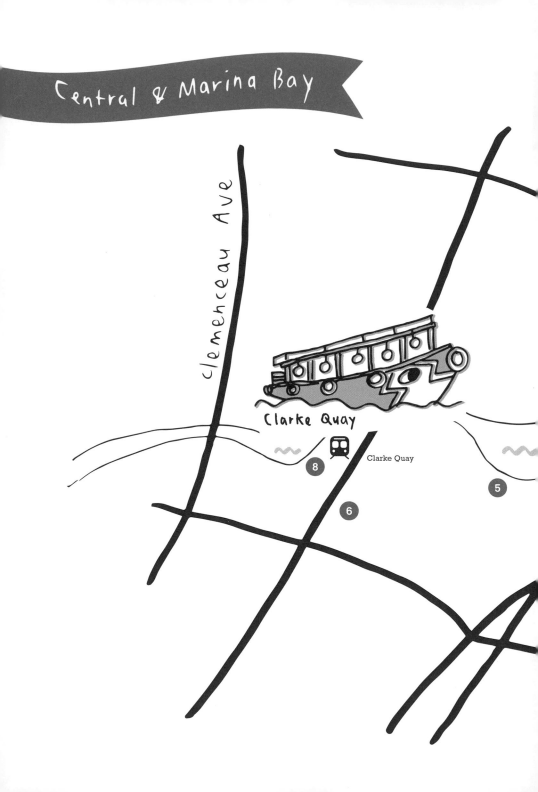

clemenceau Ave

Clarke Quay

Clarke Quay

8

6

5

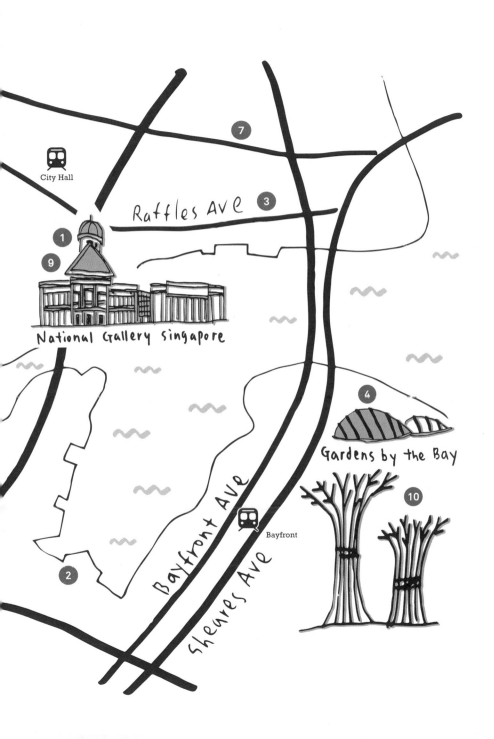

National Kitchen by Violet Oon

1 *Sophisticated Singaporean & Nyonya Cuisine*

🏠 1 St Andrew's Rd, #02-01
178957

🚃 City Hall

☎ +65 98349935

🔖 violetoon.com

✉ eat@violetoon.com

📘 National Kitchen by Violet Oon
Singapore

📷 @violetoonsingapore

🕐 Mon – Sun 12pm – 2.30pm (lunch),
3pm-5pm (tea),
6pm-10.30pm (dinner)

Violet Oon, *(read her interview on p185)*, is a Singapore national treasure, so what could be more fitting than having this wonderful chef open a restaurant in the National Gallery Singapore, providing a culinary experience to complement the artworks. Singaporean food is often relegated to being seen as simple street food, so I love how Violet has proudly bought her home recipes into the fine dining sphere. The smell of spices fills the room, hinting at the food made from scratch behind the scenes. The recipes themselves are from Violet's own experiences, using notes collected from aunties, family and friends throughout her life. Tuck into 'Tau Hu Goreng', fried bean curd with cucumber and sweet peanut sauce, classic 'Kueh Pie Tee', the Singaporean favourite 'Hainanese Chicken Rice' and 'Butter Prawns' with crispy curry leaves. Dessert is a real treat – don't miss the 'Roti Jala' a traditional Nyonya pancake with gula melaka and banana sauce. Come for lunch or dinner, and they also do an amazing afternoon tea.

Din Tai Fung

 Delicious Dumplings

🏠 #B2-05, Marina Bay Link Mall, 8A Marina Blvd, 018984

☎ +65 66347877

↖ dintaifung.com.sg

📘 Din Tai Fung Singapore

📷 @dintaifungsg

🕐 Mon – Fri 11am – 10pm

With a branch in most malls in Singapore, Din Tai Fung can be classed as a restaurant chain, but luckily in this case, it doesn't reduce the quality of the cuisine. Made with exacting standards and high levels of skill, the numerous outlets means that you're never far from the opportunity to devour some delicious dumplings. First established in Taiwan in the 1970s, the mecca of xiao long baos has since sprung up all over Asia and beyond. Its Hong Kong branch has even been awarded a one Michelin star – talk about a cheap treat! The signature dish is the steamed pork dumplings; minced pork wrapped in delicate dough, with at least 18 careful folds. Have a peek at the perfected culinary process on show through the window in the open-concept kitchen.

Dolce Vita

3 *Italian Holiday Lunch*

Some expats who live in Singapore like to bang on about brunches that they go to at weekends, with unlimited booze and piles of buffet food. For those that prefer their food not layered on top of tables, the Italian restaurant Dolce Vita at the fancy Mandarin Oriental does a slightly more civilized 'brunch'. Go strong on the starters and order French oysters, the antipasti platter with cold meats and sun-dried tomato, crab with spicy mango salsa and buffalo mozzarella and tomato salad. For mains, you can plough through pasta dishes such as gooey goats cheese and walnut orecchiette or munch on meaty slow-braised beef short rib. If you have any space for dessert, try the little raspberry panna cottas, crème brûlée and cheeses. For $158 all included, enjoy a free flow of Ruinart "R" Champagne or $118 if you're tee total.

🏠 Mandarin Oriental, 5 Raffles Ave, Marina Sq, 039797

🚇 Esplanade or Promenade

☎ +65 68853500

🏹 mandarinoriental.com/ singapore/fine-dining/ dolce-vita

✉ mosin-dining@mohg.com

📘 Mandarin Oriental Singapore

📷 @mo_singapore

🕐 Sat – Sun 12pm - 3pm (brunch)

Pollen

4 *Blooming Good Time*

If restaurants won awards for prettiest location, Pollen would be shortlisted for sure. Overlooking foxgloves and fig trees in the Mediterranean garden in the Flower Dome at Gardens by the Bay, Pollen is my top choice for afternoon tea. At $38 a head, which includes entry to the Flower Dome, it's a great choice for an outing with friends visiting from out of town. With pots of tea, and plates of cake it's hard not to imagine yourself at an Alice in Wonderland tea party, but without the Mad Hatter at your side! Everything is made in-house, from the daily baked breads to the triple chocolate brownies. Offering a great mix of savoury and sweet, scoff salmon and crème fraîche sandwiches followed by zingy passion fruit meringue tarts. Book in advance, as the terrace can be busy or sometimes closed for private events.

🏠 Flower Dome, Gardens by the Bay, 18 Marina Gardens Dr, #01-09, 018953

📞 +65 66049988

🔖 pollen.com.sg

✉️ info@pollen.com.sg

f Pollen Singapore

⌾ @pollenrestaurantsg

🕐 Afternoon tea 3pm - 5pm daily
Closed Tues

Ah Sam Cold Drink Stall

5 *Singaporean Speakeasy*

🏠 60A Boat Quay, 049848

🚉 Clarke Quay

☎ +65 65350838

📘 Ah Sam Cold Drink Stall

📷 @ahsamcolddrinkstall

🕐 Mon – Sat 6pm – 2am
Closed Sun

I don't normally hang out on Boat Quay, as it can be a bit of a tourist trap with a slightly seedy vibe, but if you are in the area I'd recommend a visit to Ah Sam Cold Drink Stall. Founded by a crew of civil servants as a hobby, when they 'thought it would be cool to have a bar', Ah Sam retains a relaxed, make-it-up-as-we-go-along atmosphere. There's no menu here, but do ask for the chocolate powdery Milo 'Tak Giu' or Kick Ball drink. This is reminiscent to the founders' childhood days at the hawker, where aunties serving Milo called the drink kick ball in response to the adverts. Other nostalgic delights include the 'Milo Dinosaur' made from egg yolk, Milo infused bourbon, port wine, and Milo powder and the 'beaded slipper', (in reference to a Peranakan dessert) made from black-spiced rum, homemade gula melaka, shredded coconut and coconut cream.

28 HongKong Street

 6 *Hidden American-style Hangout*

🏠 28 HongKong St, 059667

🚇 Clarke Quay

☎ +65 83180328

✉ findus@28hks.com

🕐 Mon - Sat 6pm - 2am
Closed Sun

Once the haunt of backpackers bunking at hostels along this stretch, HongKong Street has had a trendy revival thanks in no small part to the happening 28 HongKong Street, a serious bar hiding anonymously behind a heavy steel door. This late night hangout is inspired by bars over on America's West Coast, serving classic cocktails based with bourbons and rye. Feel all 'American adventurer' and order a 'Chevy to the levee', with High West Campfire, applejack, salted caramel, St. George spiced pear and black walnut. I personally prefer the lighter, refreshing 'Crimson and clover' with Citadelle gin, summer berries, thyme, basil and lemon. The bar snacks are awesome - I'm obsessed with the mac n cheese balls! This place is a fun watering hole to drop into after dark, and it's a welcome alternative to the rowdy beer bars nearby.

Naiise

7 *Design for Everyone*

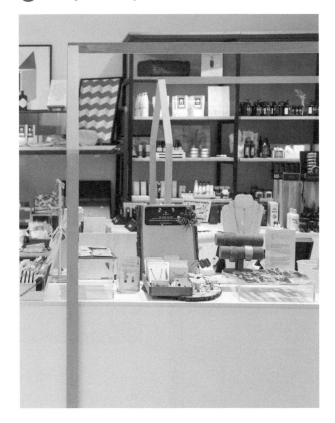

🏠 9 Raffles Boulevard, Millenia Walk, #01-42/43, 039596

🚇 Promenade

↖ naiise.com

📘 Naiise

📷 @naiise

🕐 Mon – Sun 11am – 10pm

A Singapore success story for all involved, Naiise (a Singlish play on 'nice') is a design store that began life a few years ago as an online shop and now has six brick-and-mortar spaces around the island. This is fantastic news for the many local Singaporean designers that, until Naiise came along, didn't really have an outlet to sell their unique wares. The founder Dennis started the company to provide a solution to the question, 'how could local designers reach more people?' The stores now stock more than 15,000 products from over 890 brands, with many designed or made in Singapore, keeping to its mission of promoting local design – now that's nice! Whether you're looking for deliciously smelling scented candles or colourful ceramics for your kitchen, Naiise sells something for everyone. A great place to pick up souvenirs, the Singlish phrase keyrings and Singapore Sling flavoured jams are really fun.

Ikeda Spa

8 *Japanese Spa Sanctuary*

The fifth floor of Clarke Quay Central mall might be an unlikely spot for a dreamy day spa, but as soon as you step inside the relaxing rooms at Ikeda Spa you'll be glad you wandered this way. The spa has an atmosphere of a Japanese ryokan, with subtle low lighting and warm pale woods. Book yourself in for a Zen candle therapy, where warm wax melts onto your skin in aromatherapy scents such as bamboo bliss, sakura passion and yuzu refresh. Or go for a Shiatsu acupressure, the traditional Japanese healing art designed to unblock your body's Ki (energy). The room that really makes you feel as though you've been transported to the mountains of Niseko is the onsen bathhouse made from special Hinoki, a Japanese cypress wood. Have a long soak in the steaming waters, fragranced with green tea, lavender or rose.

🏠 Clarke Quay Central,
6 Eu Tong Sen St, #05-22, 059817

🚇 Clarke Quay

☎ +65 63888080

↖ ikedaspa.com

📘 Ikeda Spa

🕐 Mon – Sun 1pm – 10pm

National Gallery Singapore

 Asian Art Collection

Launched with much fanfare to coincide with Singapore's 50th birthday in 2015, National Gallery Singapore is a huge space showcasing artworks from Singapore and Southeast Asia from the late 19th century onwards. The buildings and architecture alone are a marvel. Have a look at the holding rooms of the supreme court, and walk into the city hall chamber, also known as the surrender chamber, where in 1945, the Japanese surrendered to the allied forces. Personal favourites from the art collection include *Forest Fire*, 1811, by Raden Saleh, a pioneering Indonesian Romantic painter of Arab-Javanese ethnicity, and the works of Liu Kang, a Singapore artist famous for his Balinese themed figurative paintings and credited with creating the Nanyang Style. The gallery has a lovely shop selling items from local brands, and its awesome rooftop bar Smoke and Mirrors has a great view over the Padang.

🏠 1 St Andrew's Rd, #01-01, 178957

🚇 City Hall

📞 +65 62717000

↖ nationalgallery.sg

✉ info@nationalgallery.sg

📘 National Gallery Singapore

📷 @nationalgallerysingapore

🕐 Sun – Thurs 10am – 7pm
Fri – Sat 10am – 10pm

💲 General Admission Free, tickets required for some exhibitions

Gardens by the Bay

10 *Fantastic Flowers*

With skyscrapers rising up from almost every spare square meter of land, there have been conscious attempts to balance this and preserve Singapore's reputation as a 'Garden City'. The result is Gardens by the Bay, located behind Marina Bay Sands and occupying 101 hectares of land. While I do like scoffing sandwiches at Pollen restaurant in the Flower Dome, the Cloud Forest cooled conservatory, is one of my must-do site-seeing activities in Singapore. Developed to simulate a Southeast Asian climate based on Mount Kinabalu in Malaysia, the misty, foggy room is filled with wonderful flowers and plants from the region, including the gorgeous Rose grape Medinilla magnifica. The 35m tall waterfall is the main feature of the dome, which you can appreciate from different heights. The structure itself is stunning. Constructed using 3320 glass panels; it fits like a jigsaw, using no pillars or beams.

🏠 18 Marina Gardens Dr, 018953

🚝 Bayfront

☎ +65 64206848

↖ gardensbythebay.com.sg

f Gardens by the Bay

◎ @gardensbythebay

⌚ Mon – Sun
conservatories 9am – 9pm,
outdoor gardens 5am – 2am

💲 Conservatories $28 SGD.
Outdoor gardens are free

Bugis & Kampong Glam

Design District & Ethnic Enclaves

From the 1950s to 1980s, Bugis was famous for the gathering of glamorous transgender women who would strut up and down Bugis Street, much to the admiration of tourists and servicemen. This risqué side has since disappeared, replaced by a glut of generic malls. Luckily however, there is a growing undercurrent of art and design, with art schools, photography galleries and design stores dotted around the area.

Down the road is the iconic Raffles Hotel, a colonial charmer that's been providing beds to famous movers and shakers since 1887, with the likes of Rudyard Kipling and Somerset Maugham gracing their presence as guests.

Originally home to the Malay and Arab communities, the Kampong Glam neighbourhood continues to be a meeting point for many Muslims in Singapore. The Sultan Mosque marks the area, with its golden-topped dome glistening in the strong sun. The quirky shophouses lining Arab Street sell traditional textiles and striking silk rugs, while neighbouring Haji Lane has a vibrant mix of independent boutiques, quirky cafes, cocktail bars and tattoo parlours, which all create an alternative to the mall culture that prevails in the city.

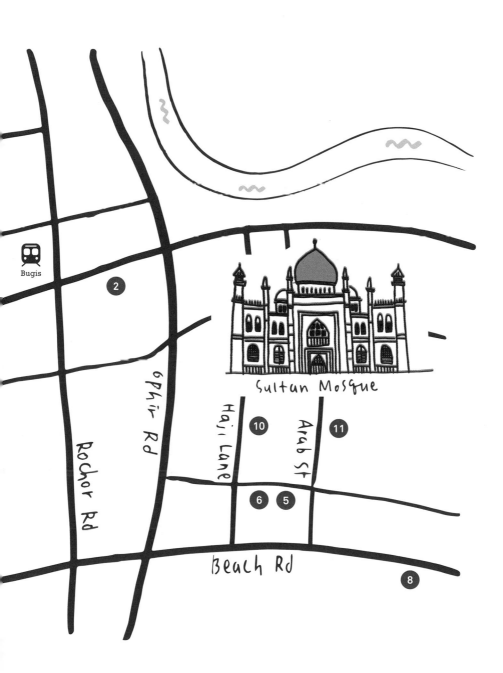

Bugis

Sultan Mosque

Ophir Rd

Rochor Rd

Haji Lane

Arab St

Beach Rd

2

10

11

6

5

8

Artichoke

1 *Middle-Eastern Munch*

Casual, unpretentious, and damn right tasty, Artichoke is a long-standing top spot for mid-week dinners and lazy weekend brunches. This Middle Eastern restaurant (without the shisha pipes) is located in an old courtyard, with leafy outdoor seating for those cooler evenings or air con inside for sweatier day times. Start with a medley of mezze - I love the smoky babaganoush sprinkled with pomegranate and the fresh figs with goats cheese is fab, along with the bright-pink beetroot tzatziki. Must-have mains include the feta burrata on Turkish toast, and the slow-roasted lamb shoulder is lovely too. The weekend brunch menu is slightly different, with more breakfasty items like huevos rancheros with avocado, beans, sausage and fried egg. While you're here, pop next door to the Objectifs photography and film centre, which often hosts small exhibitions and sells beautiful photography books by local photographers.

🏠 161 Middle Rd, 188978

🚇 Bras Basah

☎ +65 63366949

🏹 artichoke.com.sg

📘 Artichoke Singapore

📷 @artichoke_sg

🕐 Tues – Thurs 6.30pm – 10.30pm
Sat – Sun 11.30 – 3.30pm,
6.30pm-10.30pm
Closed Mon

Atlas

2 *Glamorous Gatsby-style Bar*

🏠 600 North Bridge Rd,
Parkview Square, 188778

🚇 Bugis

☎ +65 6396 4466

🔍 atlasbar.sg

✉ reservations@atlasbar.sg

📘 ATLAS Singapore

📷 @atlasbarsg

🕐 Mon – Thurs 10am – 1am
Fri 10am – 2am
Sat 3pm – 2am
Closed Sun

While I love the small and intimate speak-easy style bars in Singapore, when you want to get dressed up and go somewhere a bit more glamorous, then the glitzy Atlas bar is the place to go. Located in the impressive Parkview Square, also known locally as 'the batman building', Atlas continues the grand, 1920s-style art-deco influence in its decorations and furnishings. Specialising in gin and champagne (which was all the rage in those days), I love the 'Tamara in a Green Bugatti' with gin, lavender, lemon and mint, and the 'Atlas martini' is pretty good too! Come for the cocktails, but stay and marvel at the painstakingly replicated elegant interiors inspired by the 'Jazz Age'.

Basheer Graphic Books

(3) *Design Books & Indie Mags*

🏠 Bras Basah Complex, 231 Bain St, #04-19 180231

🚌 Bras Basah

☎ +65 63361917

✉ enquiry@basheergraphic.com

📘 Basheer Graphic Books

📷 @basheergraphic

🕐 Mon – Sat 10am – 8pm
Sun 10am – 6.30pm

Nestled discreetly on the fourth floor of the old-school Bras Basah Complex is a design lover's dream, Basheer Graphic Books. Find a treasure trove of tomes dedicated to subjects such as typography, photography, arts and crafts, architecture and interior design. Basheer started his business back in 1985, when he would go door to door selling his design books. The physical store that came afterwards was a solution to the problem at the time, when there simply weren't any bookstores for designers and artists in Singapore. A wonderful place to go for an injection of inspiration and acquire unique book titles, Basheer also has the most eclectic selection of international niche magazine titles from indie fashion and art to travel and food.

Kapok

(4) *Cool Lifestyle Concept*

🏠 National Design Centre, #01-05,
111 Middle Rd, 188969

🚇 Bugis

☎ +65 63397987

🏹 ka-pok.com

📘 kapok singapore

📷 @kapoksingapore

⊘ Mon – Sun 11am – 9pm

This cool design and lifestyle store was made with the modern, discerning and well-travelled person in mind. Originally hailing from Hong Kong, the Singapore branch is housed appropriately in the National Design Centre. Founded by Frenchman Arnaut Castel, Kapok is a welcome mix of international cult brands selling t-shirts from Kitsune and sandals from Soludos, as well as stocking bright young local brands including sustainable wrap-around trousers from Matter and stylish silk shirts from Gin Lee. The aim of the store is to champion hip and homegrown designers, supporting newcomers who might be showing their homewares or jewellery collections in a physical shop for the first time. Kapok throws community events and gatherings to foster and support local creativity. As well as selling wonderful treasures, they also have a fab little cafe called Tanuki Raw, which serves coffee, cocktails and char siew sliders.

Supermama

⑤ *Local Creator & Collaborator*

A must visit store for design devotees searching for a special souvenir, or an omiyage, as they call it in Japan, Supermama is a shining example of a company that encourages collaboration and champions local designers and heritage makers. Working together with Singaporean designers, Supermama has created close relationships with some of the best makers in Japan, in the arts of metalsmithing, porcelain-making and glassblowing. I love the delicate, ultra-thin water glasses adorned with patterns inspired by the Botanic Gardens made by Shotoku Glass, originally a light bulb manufacturer. The blue and white plates and bowls showcasing Singapore's icons are made by Kihara, a porcelain brand based in Akasaka in Japan with 400 years of history. As each item is produced using rich craftsmanship and with a strong story behind it, it's impossible not to want everything in this unique shop.

🏠 265 Beach Rd, 199544

🚇 Bugis

🔺 supermama.sg

✉ info@supermama.sg

📘 Supermama Store

📷 @supermamasg

🕐 Mon – Sun 11am – 8pm

Scene Shang

6 *Shanghai Meets Singapore in a Store*

Most new furniture in Singapore comes from designers from Europe or America, so it's an absolute delight to see the contemporary creations of Scene Shang, a local furniture brand steeped in rich Asian heritage. Pamela and Jessica (who have backgrounds in banking and interior design respectively) first met at school and continued their journey to Shanghai for work. Inspired by the East meets West and old meets new concepts they saw in China, they started to draw up plans for a modern, contemporary furniture brand with a nod to the Art Deco glam of 1930s Shanghai. Their flagship store on Beach Road is beautiful, and showcases their fabulous furniture and smaller homewares including lighting, ceramics, cushions and decorations. They also stock pieces from independent contemporary Asian designers, and hold workshops at the back of the store.

🏠 263 Beach Rd, 199542

🚇 Bugis

☎ +65 62919629

🔖 shop.sceneshang.com

📘 Scene Shang

📷 @sceneshang

🕐 Sun – Thurs 11am – 8pm
Fri – Sat 11am – 9.30pm
Closed Mon

111

Raffles Hotel

7 *Palatial Heritage Hotel*

🏠 1 Beach Rd, 189673

🚇 Esplanade

☎ +65 63371886

🏹 raffles.com/singapore

✉ singapore@raffles.com

📘 Raffles Hotel Singapore

📷 @raffleshotelsingapore

💲 From $800

One of the most iconic landmarks in Singapore, Raffles Hotel is a beautiful colonial building that has played host to the most famous and colourful of the world's characters since 1887. Past guests include Charlie Chaplin in 1931, Ava Gardener and Elizabeth Taylor in the 1950s, and Queen Elizabeth in 2006. First opened as a ten-room bungalow overlooking the beach, the hotel is a real step back in time, retaining its classic style and luxurious comfort. Even if you don't get to stay here, you can enjoy its splendour over afternoon tea, Sunday brunch in the bar and billiard room, or dinner at the Tiffin Room (a North Indian restaurant). The High Tea is a rich blend of Singaporean influences – dim sum, dumplings, chicken curry puffs and bread and butter puddings – and includes a traditional tea set with almond tarts, chocolate pralines, and coconut cake with calamansi curd.

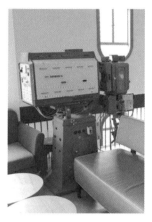

The Projector

8 *Indie Flicks*

Golden Mile Tower,
6001 Beach Rd, #05-00, 199589

Bugis

theprojector.sg

The Projector

@theprojectorsg

$13.50

Located on the fifth floor of the Golden Mile Tower, this independent cinema revives the 'Golden Theatre', which was the largest cinema in Singapore and Malaysia when it opened in 1973. The founders were frustrated; "There are so many amazing films out there every year that never get released in Singapore", so they decided to do something about it. Visitors are treated to cult favourites, fabulous foreign films as well as local films concluded with an open discussion with the director. I've watched an insightful local movie that was filmed on St. John's Island, with a Q&A with the director and actors (including an energetic elderly aunty!) afterwards. As well as beautiful Palme d'Or award winners, The Projector shows films from the Israeli film festival, to niche French and Japanese dramas, as well as British and American cult classics.

Singapore Art Museum

 Authentic Asian Art

🏠 71 Bras Basah Rd, 189555

🚇 Bras Basah

☎ +65 65899580

↖ singaporeartmuseum.sg

📘 Singapore Art Museum

📷 @singaporeartmuseum

🕐 Sat-Thurs 10am – 7pm
Fri 10am – 9pm

Of all the art galleries in Singapore, the SAM has to be one of my top choices. Founded in 1996, the gallery focuses on contemporary art from Singapore and Southeast Asia. The building space is stunning too; formerly a Catholic boys school and then a military hospital, it still retains the original chapel, with the addition of a remarkable stained-glass window. This piece, 'Quintessence', by Filipino glass sculptor Ramon Orlina, is the only art work you can touch. The gallery is designed to be an immersive experience so the installations are a range of audio, visual and video pieces with the objective of being provocative, making you think, feel and question. For someone with a short attention span like me, it's great how each room jolts you into a new experience, whether it's watching a video installation depicting life in Singapore, or walking into a white room filled with 400 vertical PVC pipes and visuals projected onto the walls. Come for the free-guided tours which happen everyday at 11am and 2pm.

Haji Lane

10 *Colourful Quirky Street*

Haji Lane stands out from the rest of Singapore's pristine shopping scene with its personality-packed, brightly coloured shophouse store fronts, intricately painted wall murals and the sound of bands playing during the evening. The boutiques are mostly independently run and filled with unique and original pieces. Women's fashion shops selling pretty dresses and blouses sourced from Seoul, a trendy **tokyobike** store, and a lively Mexican restaurant are some of the popular spots along the road. **Bar Stories** is another gem - discreetly located upstairs and decked out in mid-century furniture, it serves delicious bespoke cocktails. If you want to get your dancing shoes on, head to **Blu Jaz Cafe** for their hip-hop nights. For a much needed pamper stop by **The Nail Social**, a socially conscious salon employing and supporting underprivileged women.

🏠 Haji Ln, 189230

🚇 Bugis MRT

🕐 Shops open after midday

Arab Street

 11 *Eclectic Quarter*

Singapore is a city bursting with unique cultures from all over the world. When you're feeling that the city is slightly too slick and clean, a visit to Arab Street will shake you up a bit. Turkish restaurants and perfume shops filled with ornate bottles of jasmine and ylang ylang oils line the streets, along with Persian traders selling silk rugs.

Mamtha

A French friend of mine told me about a wonderful woman called Mamtha, a go-to person for anyone interested in meditation and healing. Located in a simple loft room on the second floor of a shophouse, her space is filled with crystals, Tibetan bowls and tarot cards. Come here for a reviving meditation session, or relax while making brightly coloured mandala.

🏠 23A Arab St, 199722

☎ +65 97499287

➹ taralightwithin.com

Dilip Textiles

Although there are lots of lovely fabric shops in and around Arab Street, I always come to Dilip Textiles to get beautiful, affordable, printed, colourful cushions and fabrics for my home or for presents. Sourced in India, they also sell table cloths, bedspreads and the cosiest quilts.

🏠 74 Arab St, 199771

Maison Ikkoku

A cafe by day and a cocktail bar by night, Maison Ikkoku is a discreet hangout that is great to visit after 7pm, when you can see the Sultan Mosque lit up, and hear the soothing sounds of the Islamic Call to Prayer.

🏠 20 Kandahar St, 198885

🔖 maison-ikkoku.net

Cichetti

Charming and cosy, Cichetti is a fabulous, low-key Italian restaurant on Kandahar Street, with a roaring wood-fired oven taking centre stage. The antipasti are divine – pick at plates of burratina, beef carpaccio and roasted pumpkin.

🏠 52 Kandahar St, 198901

🔖 cicheti.com

Little India & Jalan Besar

Vibrant and Colourful Community

An antithesis to how Singapore is typically seen, the Little India neighbourhood feels a bit more like Mumbai – chaotic, colourful and charming. Along the streets you'll see women sashaying in bright-pink saris, stalls selling sweet-smelling jasmine meticulously handmade into garlands and stacks of vibrant vegetables such as purple eggplants and green gourds spilling onto the pavement. Take a moment to listen to the vivacious music blaring out from the mini marts tuned into local Hindu radio stations. Admire and observe the vibrant crowds at festivals, such as Thaipusam early on in the year, or Deepavali, the Hindu festival of light come autumn. Catch the latest Bollywood blockbuster at the cinema, followed by a spicy curry or southern Indian style thosai.

Parallel to Little India's Serangoon road is Jalan Besar. This area is known for its streets of hardware stores selling everything including the kitchen sink, alongside machinery repair shops and garages. Cool coffee shops and creative studios have now sprung up, adding a hip edge to this industrial area.

Little India & Jalan Besar

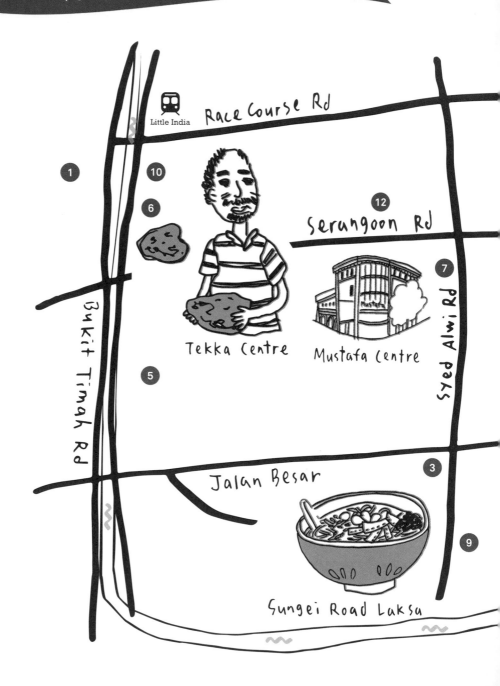

Little India

Race Course Rd

Serangoon Rd

Bukit Timah Rd

Syed Alwi Rd

Jalan Besar

Tekka Centre

Mustafa Centre

Sungei Road Laksa

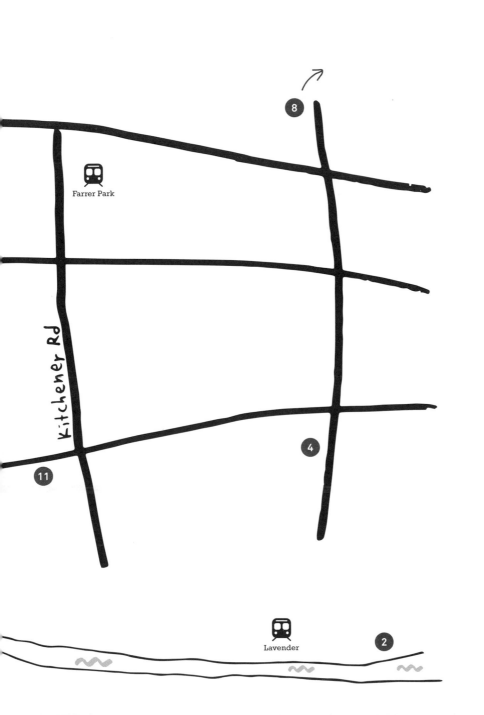

Wild Rocket

① *Creative Singaporean Cuisine*

Run by the charismatic chef Willin Low, Wild Rocket is a brilliant restaurant that serves Modern Singaporean food. A lawyer by trade, Willin is a self-taught chef, who began his culinary foray moonlighting as a chef-for-hire at the weekends. Since giving up his previous day job over a decade ago, he's now firmly made a name for himself on the Singapore food scene. Go for the chef's Omakase menu served at the counter where you'll be treated to dishes such as Thai pomelo salad with king prawns and coconut ice cream, nasi lemak with Hokkaido scallop, and laksa risotto with honey and sea urchin. The chef jokes that overseas they always have 'Singapore fried noodle' on the menu in Chinese restaurants (although such a dish doesn't exist) so he's added it to his menu for fun. The desserts are delightful; try the sorbet with pink guava (an ode to the pink guava tree his grandma had in her garden), and the pandan infused panna cotta with salted gula melaka.

🏠 10A Upper Wilkie Rd, 288119

🚇 Little India

☎ +65 63399448

🔦 wildrocket.com.sg

📘 Wild Rocket

📷 @willcookwilleat

🕐 Mon – Sat 12pm – 3pm, 6.30pm – 10.30pm
Closed Sun

Kilo

2 *Far-Flung Food Joint*

I love the location of Kilo; perched over the Kallang River, it feels like you're in the middle of nowhere. There are two restaurants here - the original Kilo on the fourth floor and its hip younger brother Camp Kilo on the ground floor – both equally worth a visit. I am always interested in the history of buildings, and so was intrigued to learn that this was once a Malaysian customs office. Goods would be loaded and unloaded having been transported up the river, and the cargo lift is still in place, taking hungry diners up to Kilo. Both restaurants are best experienced with a group of friends, especially as this will allow you to try more items on the menu. At Kilo, I adore the wasabi tuna tartare, the crispy soft-shell crab and the squid ink rice with one of their cucumber cocktails. At Camp Kilo it's all about the fresh-off-the-grill meat-meals, such as crispy pork belly and roast chicken with jerk spices followed by dulche de leche for dessert.

🏠 66 Kampong Bugis, 338987

🚇 Lavender

☎ +65 64673987

↖ kilokitchen.com

✉ reservations@kilokitchen.com or campkilo@kilokitchen.com

📘 Kilo & Camp Kilo Charcoal Club

📷 @kilokitchen & @campkilo

🕐 **Kilo:** Mon – Sat 6pm – 12am
   Closed Sun

   Camp Kilo: Fri 5.30pm – 11pm
   Sat-Sun 11am – 11pm
   Mon – Thurs Closed

Jalan Besar Food

 Neighbourhood Nibbles

Sungei Road Laksa

Many an argument has been had about where you can find the best laksa in Singapore. I don't claim to have the answer, but my vote goes to the small and authentic charcoal cooked laksa in this little kopitiam in Jalan Besar. I assure you, this bowl will be one of the best $3 you will spend during your time in Singapore!

27 Jalan Berseh, #01-100
Jin Shui Kopitiam, 200027

Thurs – Tues 9.30am – 5pm
Closed Wed

The Refinery

A spacious cafe and lunch spot located in an old, airy warehouse, The Refinery serves a Japanese-inspired menu with generous portions, at an affordable price. Go for one of their signature rice bowls, such as the 'teriyaki chicken don' ($14) with fried chicken skin and 72-degree onsen egg, and order a side of tempura to share.

115 King George's Avenue
#01-02, 208561

Tues – Fri 12pm – 11pm
Sat 11am – 12pm
Sun 11am – 4pm
Closed Mon

Swee Choon Tim Sum

Back-alley dining at its best, Swee Choon is a must visit for its bustling atmosphere and damn tasty dim sum, transporting your taste buds to the streets of Hong Kong and Shanghai. Great for groups, order up a stack of steamer cases full of freshly prepared xiao long bao and char siew bao. They're also famous for their Portuguese egg tarts.

183-191 Jalan Besar, 208882

Mon - Sat 11am-2.30pm, 6pm-6am
Sun 10am - 3pm, 6pm-6am
Closed Tues

Chye Seng Huat Hardware

4 *The Best Beans*

🏠 150 Tyrwhitt Rd, 207563

🚇 Lavender

↖ cshhcoffee.com

📘 Chye Seng Huat Hardware

📷 @cshhcoffeee

🕐 Tues – Thurs 9am – 10pm
Fri – Sat 9am – 12am
Sun 9am – 10pm
Closed Mon

Originally one of the many hardware stores found in Jalan Besar, CSHH is now a destination stop for caffeine geeks. The shop is run by Papa Palheta, an independent roaster and supplier of coffee in Singapore and Malaysia. This buzzing and busy cafe serves seasonal single origins brewed by the cup, and for those extra sizzling days you can order a cold brew on a nitro tap. Take home your own bag of Papa Palheta beans from their in-house shop, which also sells coffee equipment such as AeroPress coffee and espresso makers. Those serious about learning more about the black beans can sign up to classes at the C-Platform or attend a one-hour roasting tour, which provides insight into the science and art of roasting coffee beans. A cool space to check out, CSHH is housed in an art deco shophouse, retaining many of its original features, and has a cactus filled courtyard that gets lively come evening.

Meatsmith Little India

5 *Spiced-up American BBQ*

I love the curry houses and vegetarian restaurants that are dotted around this neighbourhood, but for something completely quirky and out of the box, Meatsmith Little India is one to check out. Part of the same family as Burnt Ends and Meatsmith (on Telok Ayer St), this place was born out of a love of barbecue culture blended with the tastes of India. Infused with the spices and herbs sourced from nearby Tekka Centre, the meat is grilled, smoked and roasted on the wood-fire flames or in the tandoor oven. This is a top spot for groups and parties as the flavoursome food is great for sharing. For starters, the 'Madras pork cheeks' are addictive, and for mains be sure to order the 'bone marrow curry' and the 'biryani-stuffed suckling pig'. Upstairs is their bar Rogue Trader (you can eat up here too), a colonial-inspired bar serving the most inventive gin and tonics – I like the one with fresh curry leaves and pink peppercorns!

🏠 21 Campbell Lane, 209894

🚇 Little India

☎ +65 9625 9056

↖ meatsmith.com.sg

✉ littleindia@meatsmith.com.sg

f Meatsmith Little India

⊙ @roguetrader_sg

⊘ Tues-Fri 5pm – 11.30pm
Sat – Sun 11.30am – 11.30pm
Closed Mon

Tekka Centre

6 *Authentic Asian Market*

Southeast Asia is known for its bustling wet markets, which are often a focal point of the community. While modern western-style supermarkets have replaced many of these traditional markets, a couple like Tekka Centre (and Tiong Bahru Market) have remained, helping to maintain the local charm of their neighbourhoods. I love the banana leaf stalls, run by enterprising women wearing elegant bright saris (who'd have thought the demand for banana leaves was so high it would warrant dedicated stalls!). In the dry section, you'll find curry powder pastes, dried anchovy and shrimp. Fresh fish is loaded onto tables, and big butcher's blocks sit to the side, where you'll find men chopping slabs of goat meat. A fabulous place to pick up fruit; make sure you try the local yellow jackfruit and the marvellous mangosteen. There's also a hawker centre section with food stalls, ranging from roti prata to biryani to chendol, and drinks stalls offering big green coconuts and raw cane sugar.

 665 Buffalo Rd, 210665

Little India

Mon – Sun 6.30am – 9pm

Mustafa Centre

7 *Round-the-Clock Everything Shop*

A mecca for shopping lovers, Mustafa Centre is open daily, day and night and has everything you could ever ask for under one roof. Six floors full of stuff, departments range from a full-blown supermarket to an electronics store, rooms containing rails of clothes to useful toiletries on the ground floor. I particularly like the textiles section in basement one where you'll see row upon row of fabric rolls in snazzy metallic purples, golds and greens. The sari fabrics are stunning - find metres of chiffon with intricate silver beading and embroidery. Just to warn you - it's easy to get carried away at Mustafa. On my last visit, after a late dinner at Swee Choon, I walked out at 11pm with a garden hose (that I definitely needed!).

 145 Syed Alwi Rd, 207704

Farrer Park

mustafa.com.sg

Mon – Sun Open 24 hours

Hock Siong & Co.

8 *Flea-Market Style Homeware Shop*

Whenever I visit a new city or even a country village, I'll always track down the local second hand shops or flea markets to scour for the most unusual finds. Hock Siong started off in the 1970s as a 'Karung Guni' family business of rag and bone traders. They take second-hand furniture from house clearance and hotels and sell it to the public for reasonable prices. The stock varies from day to day, but expect to find everything from a collection of white and blue ceramic rice cups from a chicken and rice restaurant to pastel hued enamel tin bowls and traditional Chinese urns, to dial-up landline phones. I like coming here for their rows of lamps with lovely oriental designs (looks like they're from hotel rooms). Located in an old industrial building, Hock Siong & Co is slightly out of the way and might be hard to get to using public transport, but it's an easy taxi ride away from the centre of town.

153 Kampong Ampat, 368326

Tai Seng

+65 62818338

hocksiong.com.sg

Hock Siong & Co.

@hocksiong

Mon – Sun 9.30am – 5.45.pm

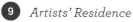

The Vagabond Club

9 *Artists' Residence*

A delight for art lovers, The Vagabond Club is a luxurious boutique hotel in Jalan Besar, and a stone's throw away from Little India and Kampong Glam. Loud to say the least, the lobby is filled with pillar-box red sofas, glistening gold trees and walls jam-packed with paintings, photography and curated artworks. Check in is at a rhino reception desk, made by the Allahbusksh family in India (who make armoury for Rajasthan royalty) The 42 rooms are wonderfully cosy and packed with personality, with interesting ornaments, rich homely fabrics and walls covered with travel photography. French designer Jacques Garcia designed the hotel, so there's a Parisian touch to the elegant and welcoming rooms. A champion for art, the hotel has an artist-in-residence programme, hosting writers, poets, musicians and artists. I love the area too - you're a short walk away from amazing local food around Jalan Besar.

🏠 39 Syed Alwi Rd, 207630

🚉 Lavender

☎ +65 62916677

↖ hotelvagabondsingapore.com

✉ info@hotelvagabondsingapore.com

📘 The Vagabond Club

📷 @thevagabondclub

💲 From $275

Little India

10 *Cultural Neighbourhood*

Moghul Sweet Shop

Located in Little India Arcade, Moghul is an addictive discovery. Selling the most amazing Northern Indian sweets, I love the milk cake and the coconut ladoo with dried fruits. To call them sweet is an understatement, but they are delightful and also affordable, from $1 per piece.

Little India Arcade, 48 Serangoon Rd, #01-16, 217959

Nalli Silks & Sarees

If I were invited to an Indian wedding, I'd pay a visit to Nalli to get fitted for such an occasion. Even if said invitation is still waiting in the post, I urge you to go see this wonderful shop for its beautiful fabrics with pretty prints that can be used for decoration as well as for dressing. The intricate embroidery work is stunning - I'm currently eyeing up the thick raw silks in silvers, reds and greens for some DIY home decor.

 10 Buffalo Rd, 219784

Jothi Store & Flower Shop

I love finding those small shops that seemingly sells everything - Jothi Store is one of these. As well as selling fragrant flowers, they've got cool homewares such as copper water cups and metal embossed plates. They also stock the amazing Ayurvedic brand Indian Himalaya Herbals, which has the best lip balms and shampoos!

 1 Campbell Ln, 209882

Khansama

A visit to Little India isn't complete without ordering a few dishes at the delightful Khansama. I get withdrawal symptoms if I go too long without their signature aloo tikki chaat with chickpeas.

166 Serangoon Rd, 218050

Mud Rock Ceramics

11 *Creative Ceramic Classes*

'Happily handmade ceramics' is how duo Michelle Lim and Ng Seok Har describe their creative studio. Although they are kept thoroughly busy producing bespoke collections for restaurants, design companies and architecture firms, they somehow find the time to do classes for regular folk. During the class, these lovely ladies will show you how to firstly prepare the clay, and then mould bowls at the wheel. They then fire your pieces in their own kilns and finish with a glaze. Luckily Michelle and Seok are patient teachers - even when your formation falls flat on the wheel. Ask the girls about their involvement with Singapore's present to Queen Elizabeth II for her 90th birthday. They created a beautiful turquoise tea set - a prototype of which can be seen in the studio. Michelle told me how she ended up carrying the final piece personally on a flight to London, in order to ensure its safety!

🏠 85 Maude Rd, 208357

🚇 Farrer Park

🏹 mudrockceramics.com

✉️ mudrockceramics@gmail.com

📷 @mudrockceramics

⊘ Classes Saturday 11 – 1.30pm
or 2.30 – 5pm
Thurs 7pm-9.30pm by appointment

Sri Veeramakaliamman Temple

12 *Vibrant Tamil Temple*

India must be one of the most culturally rich and interesting places that I've ever visited, and a morning at this temple gives you a tiny taste of the vibrant country. Singapore's oldest Hindu temple is dedicated to the goddess Kali, the destroyer of evil. It is said that in the early days, it was an important gathering point for migrant workers from India who came here to worship and pray to feel safe in a new, foreign land. It soon became the focal point of the Indian community in Singapore along Serangoon road. At first sight, the 'Rajagopuram' (tower) is awe-inspiring, with colourful statues displaying Hindu stories. Sunday is the busiest day, where you can discreetly observe the prayer and blessing rituals of this community.

141 Serangoon Rd, 218042

Little India

sriveeramakaliamman.com

Mon – Sun 5.30am – 9.30pm

135

East Coast

Charming Coastal Suburb

Oh, the East Coast! If you're staying in the centre of Singapore, getting to this quaint 'hood can feel like a hassle, but it's worth the journey, especially as you can spend all day here – cycling under swaying palms along the beach, wandering past pretty Peranakan houses and sampling the local snacks. As a nostalgia nerd, I love the old-fashioned feel of the low-rise neighbourhood of Joo Chiat, characterised by delightful shophouses in pastel-blues, peachy-oranges and pale-pink hues. Walk past old warehouses stocking stacks of flour, and soak up the interesting mix of cultures, from the Buddhist temples to the Muslim mosques.

    Compared to the city centre, life feels slower here. These charming neighbourhoods have a friendly community feel, and the breezy coastline is lovely for a long walk, or alternatively, more physical activities such as water skiing or paddle boarding. The East Coast Park links to Marina Barrage, and onto Marina Bay, so you can easily hop on a bike and peddle into town in no time, making this area feel more accessible.

Old Airport Road
Food Centre

3

Paya Lebar

East coast parkway

Eunos

Sims Ave

Geylang Rd

Joo Chiat Rd

Koon Seng Road

Still Rd

East Coast Rd

East Coast Park

Mr and Mrs Mohgan's Super Crispy Roti Prata

① *South Indian Style Breakfast*

Regarded by some as serving up the most perfect prata in Singapore, this place on the corner of Crane Road in Joo Chiat is well worth a visit for an authentic, old-school and great value breakfast. Run by Mr and Mrs Mohgan, who have been making this dish for more than 30 years, I suggest coming early in the morning to get your fuel for the day. Order their delicious roti prata – a south Indian-style fried pancake - poured over a flat grill, with a side of curry. Crispy on the outside, while fluffy and soft on the inside, it comes plain or with egg and onion. Located in a traditional open-air kopitiam, pull up a plastic chair on the pavement to devour your dish. Best to come mid-week if possible, as this popular joint becomes quite crowded on weekends.

🏠 7 Crane Rd, 429356

🚇 Paya Lebar

🕐 Thurs – Mon 6.30am – 1.30pm
Closed Tue – Wed

Chin Mee Chin Confectionery

Charming Coffee Shop

②

As cities around the world become obsessed with creating identikit cafes with industrial lighting and recycled wooden furniture, Chin Mee Chin Confectionery (CMCC) is a welcoming breath of fresh air with its original green and white tiled floors and marble-topped kopitiam tables behind a traditional open-air shop front. Setting up shop in the 1960s, regulars to CMCC will tell you how they used to come here as children and how it hasn't changed much since then, and I think it's all the better for it. Run by a group of bubbly women, the charming cafe is famous for its ($1!) kaya toast served on a round bun (making it unique to CMCC). Their creamy custard tarts and freshly baked cupcakes are worth a try too. Grab a cup of kopi before venturing off for a leisurely cycle ride along East Coast Park just down the road.

🏠 204 East Coast Rd, 428903

🚇 Paya Lebar or Eunos

🕐 Tues – Sun 8.30am – 4pm
Closed Mon

Old Airport Road Food Centre

 Foodie Favourite

A one-stop shop for a medley of superb food, Old Airport Road Food Centre is a much-loved culinary stomping ground for locals, and an absolute must do for visitors.

 51 Old Airport Rd, 390051

Dakota

Mon – Sun 8am – 12am

Roast Paradise

Set up by young and passionate Gen Y hawkers after doing an apprenticship at a stall in Kuala Lumpur, Roast Paradise sells delicious Chinese-style char siew, honey BBQ pork and caramelised sweet roasted pork dishes. Follow them on insta @roastparadise for mouth-watering updates!

 #01-122, Old Airport Rd Food Centre

Soursop Juice (Lim Hin)

This soursop stall has been around for over 30 years (in various locations), and continues to churn out the highest quality pulpy juice, using soursop fruit grown locally in Southeast Asia.

 #01-36, Old Airport Rd Food Centre

Home-Made Pau Specialist

Around the corner from the main food centre, in Mui Thiang Kee Eating House in Cassis Cresent, is the humble but brilliant home-made pau specialist. Order plates of pau filled with BBQ pork, their specialty siew mai pork dumplings or their signature coffee pau, with coffee and lotus paste.

 Blk 34 Cassia Cresent #01-86, (Old Airport Rd) 390034

Long Phung

4 *Fantastic Pho*

🏠 159 Joo Chiat Rd, 427436

🚇 Paya Lebar or Eunos

☎ +65 64406959

↖ longphungvietrest.com

🕐 Mon – Sun 12pm – 10pm

Joo Chiat Road has a variety of Vietnamese restaurants, all serving good value, fresh, filling food with Long Phung being one of the best along this stretch. With a similar vibe to eateries found in Saigon, Long Phung is a casual, no frills spot, with bright yellow plastic chairs, and simple decor. Order a bowl of $7 pho, or delicious chicken noodle soup along with goi cuon prawn spring rolls with a side of sweet sauce, and sip on a thick mango smoothie or a cold fresh coconut. A good place for a lunch stop while wandering around the East Coast area, be sure to come early as the queue builds up at around midday.

Hat of Cain

(5) *Stylish Hand-Woven Hats*

With it being sunny most days in Singapore, you're going to want to take shade under a stylish hat. Cue Hat of Cain, the purveyors of Panama hats perfect for the tropical climate. The showroom is set up in a charming shophouse, decorated with retro desk lamps and oil paintings, with the hats displayed in dark wooden cabinets. Set up by long-term expat Bill Cain, the shop specialises in authentic, hand-woven Panama hats from Ecuador. Catering to both men and women, 'The Plantation' style hat is my top pick, a wide brimmed hat that I wear on the beach with a bikini or at a wedding with a jumpsuit. You'll need to organise your visit, as the shop is open only on Saturdays, or you can arrange an evening appointment after 6pm. The personal service and knowledge from the owner is worth a trip here!

🏠 18 Joo Chiat Ter, 427186

🚏 Paya Lebar

☎ + 65 88096242

↖ hatofcain.com

f Hat of Cain

⦿ @hatofcain

⊘ Saturday 11am – 5pm
Evenings after 6pm by appointment

Stale & Co

6 *Joo Chiat Jeweller*

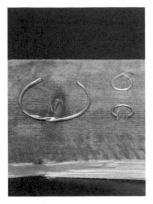

One of my favourite secret finds in Singapore is the silversmith Stale & Co located discreetly on the third floor of a building on Joo Chiat Road. Run by duo Daryl and Stella, the studio is part metal workshop, part showroom, with rows of pliers, cups of clasps, soldering irons and boxes of tools on the worktops where the industrious pair work. 'Handsome metal things' is how they describe their wares, and I couldn't agree more. Made in-house from scratch using ancient techniques, the sterling silver jewellery of chunky rings and heavy battered cuff bracelets sit alongside more delicate pieces. They also accept commissioned work - check out their instagram @staleandco to see the most awesome and unique wedding bands, or his and hers spiral cuffs.

🏠 237C Joo Chiat Rd, 427494

🚇 Paya Lebar

➤ staleandco.com

✉ info@staleandco.com

⬜ Stale & Co

⭕ @staleandco

⊘ by appointment

Cat Socrates

7 *Locally-sourced Curiosities*

A quirky and quaint shop located along Joo Chiat Road, Cat Socrates is a room full of curiosities, collectables and of course the odd cat! A fun place to pick up local Singapore souvenirs, its shelves are piled high with colourful Peranakan-style tiles, locally inspired hand-illustrated postcards, books on Singlish as well as Singaporean literature, jars of homomade jam, prints and posters of chophouses and tote bags printed with Singapore icons such as the durian fruit. A toyshop for both adults and children is how I would describe it; Cat Socrates also stocks hip homewares, like terrariums to house your own mini green garden. Catering to the creative souls, they also have a shop tucked away in Bras Basah, near Bugis.

🏠 448 Joo Chiat Rd, 427661

🚇 Paya Lebar

☎ +65 63480863

🔖 catsocrates.com.sg

📷 @cat_socrates

🕐 Tues - Sun 12.30pm - 9.30pm
Closed Mon

147

East Coast Park

(8) *Beachside Coastal Park*

A 15km stretch of park and beach, the East Coast is a perfect choice for a long Saturday cycle session. Get a taxi to drop you off at East Coast Parkway and rent a bicycle, or if you're feeling romantic, a tandem bike for two. Lifestyle Bike N Skate rents out a bike for $12 for three hours (remember to bring ID, as they require it). Pedal past volleyball players on the sand, and large container ships floating out in the Singapore Straits in the distance. Push on for 12 or so kilometers and you will reach Marina Barrage (keep your eyes open for otters; I've seen them waddle out of the water and hang out on the grassy bank). This lovely route will take you through Gardens by the Bay, finishing your journey at Marina Bay. For a tasty snack I recommend stopping at Satay by the Bay for delicious coal-grilled meaty-skewers with peanut sauce.

 1030 East Coast Parkway, 449893

Kembangan

Koon Seng Road

(9) *Colourful Heritage Homes*

Sightseeing in Singapore can often involve searching for heritage houses. Some of the finest, brightest examples of this can be seen along Koon Seng Road, in the Joo Chiat area. Built in the 1920s, and originally home to the Peranakan community who clustered here, these candy-hued houses are absolutely charming and amazingly well preserved. Start at no. 21 Koon Seng Road and wander down from door to door while admiring the rainbow of façades and the floral tiles set in the walls. I particularly like the pink house with olive green painted wooden shutters with windows surrounded by decorative tiles. Koon Seng Road is a great spot for that picture postcard shot of old Singapore.

🏠 Koon Seng Rd, 426969

🚇 Paya Lebar

South & Outdoors

Wild & Wonderful

The real appeal of Singapore, aside from the fantastic food, is the many places that remind you of the city's former life as a peaceful, sleepy backwater; the city of old where a couple of kampung villages was all that existed on this tropical island one degree (140km) north of the equator.

Today patchworks of parks weave through the developed urban sprawl, with leafy lungs in the centre starting at MacRitchie Reservoir Park, past Singapore Zoo and moving north towards the border of Malaysia. Here, quiet corners of countryside remain, and if you hop on a boat to Pulau Ubin Island, you can seemingly step back in time to get a glimpse of Singapore's former laid-back life. Closer to the heart of the city centre, you'll find wild walkways such as the Southern Ridges which lead you to parks dotted around the south of Singapore. Break up your walk with a visit to Gillman Barracks, a brilliant art enclave, with a rotation of inspiring contemporary works by Asian artists.

Hop over the bridge or jump in the cable car from HarbourFront to the resort island of Sentosa, which is filled with theme parks and golf courses and offers breezy coastal stretches for a lazy sunny day under a swaying palm tree.

South & Outdoors

Gillman Barracks

Jurong Island

MacRitchie Reservoir

HarbourFront

Sentosa

Tanjong Beach Club

Tanjong Beach Club

1 *Sunny Seaside Spot*

A sun-kissed playground for all ages, Tanjong Beach Club is a go-to destination in Sentosa, as island off the south coast of Singapore, for those wanting to escape the urban centre and spend the day on a palm-fringed sandy beach. Gather a group of friends and bag yourself a daybed near the shore. The food here is fab - I'd go for snapper ceviche with avocado and cucumber, and order the TBC seafood platter with oysters, lobster and crab to share. Sip on cool cocktails such as the sunset daiquiri with mango and papaya, and the piña coladas that come in a whole pineapple fruit! For those more active, there's beach volleyball and stand-up paddleboards for hire along the beach. This place gets packed at the weekends, so call ahead to reserve or come during the week when it's less busy and the vibe is more laid-back.

120 Tanjong Beach Walk,
Sentosa Island, 098942

HarbourFront

+65 97505323

tanjongbeachclub.com

Tanjong Beach Club

@tanjongbeachclub

Tues - Fri 11am - 10pm
Sat - Sun 10am - 11pm
Closed Mon

Tamarind Hill

2 *Delightful Thai*

You can probably tell by now that I've got a serious soft spot for well-preserved heritage buildings, with the restaurant at Tamarind Hill being one of the finest examples. A truly Southeast Asian experience, this authentic Thai restaurant sits in a beautiful bungalow on the edge of a leafy park. The old house has been restored and lovingly decorated with antique furniture and vintage Northern Thai textiles from the Angkla tribe. Sit outside on the veranda, and order a feast of tom yum soup, deep fried dumplings and beef massaman curry. The bar in the centre of the bungalow is super charming, serving cocktails infused with local flavours such as the lychee lemongrass smash and Siam sun rays, served in bamboo cups. They do a great value Sunday brunch here - $60 for any dishes that you like - it's amazing. After lunch, head down through Labrador Park to the Dragon's Teeth Gate, once a famous hideout for pirates.

🏠 30 Labrador Villa Rd, 119189

🚇 Labrador Park

☎ +65 62786364

➤ tamarindrestaurants.com

📘 Tamarind Hill Singapore

📷 @samadhi_retreats

⏱ Mon - Sun 12am - 3pm, 6pm - 11pm

Col Bar

3 *Old School Beer Bar*

🏠 9A Whitchurch Rd, 138839

🚇 One North

🕐 Tues - Sat 11am - 10pm
Closed Mon

A complete contrast to the swanky cocktail bars that have popped up on the Singapore bar scene, Col Bar is a seriously old school spot set in the jungle-like Portsdown Road area. With its blue painted walls, and photos of sports teams hung on the wall, it feels more like a Boy Scouts' club than a pub. Col Bar, short for 'colonial bar', originally opened in the 1950s as a canteen for the British army. The decor hasn't changed much, only adding to its nostalgic charm. Still catering to the English tastes, you can order marmite sandwiches as well as greasy fry-ups and traditional fish and chips. For booze, your choice is bottles of beer or fruity ciders, which you help yourself to from the fridge. Col Bar is always a favourite with friends who live in or come to visit Singapore.

Capella Singapore

Lush Hotel Hideaway

Away from the busy city on Sentosa, the Capella Singapore hotel is a smart, sprawling jungle escape looking out over the sea. Stay in one of the rooms for a real treat, or alternatively, visit one of their lovely restaurants. A popular staycation destination in Singapore, bedrooms have big bathrooms, and views over a panel of green ancient trees outside your window. A lesser-known tip is their amazing afternoon tea at Cassia. Settle down on the quiet terrace and order the oriental dim sum with steamed siew mai topped with sea urchin or steamed lobster dumpling, or the more traditional colonial afternoon tea with lemon tart meringue and green tea pound cake. As a guest you've got access to numerous pools spread out over the landscape: I like the smaller lap pool hidden away down at the bottom of the hill. For both guests and non-guests, The Knolls does a fantastic Sunday brunch, which is great for groups. Finish up at Bob's Bar for Bloody Marys.

🏠 1 The Knolls, Sentosa Island, 098297

🚉 HarbourFront

☎ +65 63778888

🔗 capellahotels.com

📘 Capella Singapore

📷 @capellasin

💲 From $680

Gillman Barracks

5 *Amazing Art*

Built in 1936 for use by the British Army, Gillman Barracks now has a new lease of life, being home to a of wonderful group of galleries championing Singaporean and Southeast Asian art. There are monthly events such as 'Art Day Out' or 'Art After Dark' where the galleries put on workshops and talks as well as film screenings and theatre performances. Located directly on the Southern Ridges walking trail, this is a great stop-off point during your hike, making a wholesome day of nature and art.

Yeo Workshop

Owner Audrey Yeo does a fabulous job of curating interesting work from emerging and experimental artists from Singapore and the Asian region. Past shows include sculptural installations, cutting edge videos and contemporary paintings by artist from Singapore, Vietnam and China respectively.

🏠 1 Lock Rd #01-01, 108932

↖ yeoworkshop.com

Mizuma

First established in Tokyo during the 1990s, Mizuma opened its doors in Singapore with the aim of promoting Japanese artists to the region while highlighting young talent from Southeast Asia to the international art scene.

🏠 22 Lock Rd #01-34, 108939

↖ mizuma.sg

NTU CCA

The NTU Centre for Contemporary Art is an important gallery to Singapore. It is a research centre that holds exhibitions, residencies and research, encouraging critical discourse and experimental contemporary art practices.

Block 43 Malan Rd, 109443

ntu.ccasingapore.org

The Naked Finn

Serving seafood with soul, The Naked Finn is a great dinner spot located discreetly in the Gillman Barracks enclave. Ken, the restaurant's founder, has a fascinating approach to sourcing, whereby he introduces non-mainstream species of seafood into the kitchen, thereby working towards a more sustainable supply chain. Sample baby squid carpaccio, scallops from Hokkaido and mesclun salad grown locally in Singapore.

 Block 39 Malan Rd, 109442

 nakedfinn.com

Creamier

You're bound to get a bit hot wandering around the Gillman Barracks art block, but thankfully Creamier is on hand to help you cool off. Serving up the sweetest smelling waffles, with dollops of local flavours like tau sar piah, sea salt gula melaka and mango passion fruit. They produce their artisanal ice creams on-site in small batches, so it's super fresh.

5A Lock Rd, 108927

creamier.com.sg

The Southern Ridges

6 *Wild Panoramic Walkway*

The Southern Ridges hiking trail is a wonderful way to see a slice of Singapore, one of the reasons being is that you seamlessly meander along the green spaces sandwiched between the ever-growing urban developments. Start at HarbourFront MRT and follow the sign-posted path through thick lush greenery, where you will experience stunning panoramic views over the city and the sea. Wander along clever walkways and climb across cool bridges – the Henderson Waves bridge is an awesome wooden wonder! Be sure to stop by Gillman Barracks on your way for a dose of art and ice cream. Another lovely option is to end up at Tamarind Hill in Labrador Park for a Thai lunch. The total route is 10km but you can easily start and stop depending on how long you want to go for.

🏠 Marang Rd, 098867

🚋 HarbourFront

↖ nparks.gov.sg

MacRitchie Reservoir

(7) *Jungle Jaunt*

A short ten-minute drive away from the city centre is the start of an 11km scenic nature trail around the reservoir at MacRitchie. Round up some friends, stock up on bottles of water and snacks, and venture along wooden boardwalks, past cool-water lakes, and into the dense lush greenery of the forest. Keep your eyes peeled for mischievous monkeys and the occasional slithering snake, and if you're lucky you might spy a rare scaly pangolin. Make your way to the highlight of the three-hour hike, a 250m freestanding suspension bridge known as the TreeTop Walk. Here, you'll get a bird's-eye view and perfect photo opportunity of the forest canopy and blue reservoir.

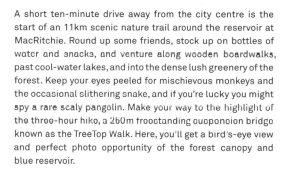

🏠 Reservoir Rd, 570000

🚇 Caldecott

➤ nparks.gov.sg

📷 @nparksbuzz

⊘ Mon – Sun 7am - 7pm

Kebun Baru Birdsinging Club

8 *Singapore Songbirds*

Kebun Baru is one of the last surviving bird singing clubs, a traditional and unique activity in Singapore. As the name suggests, this place attracts bird enthusiasts, but not just any birds – these are singing birds, which their owners pay hundreds, if not thousands, of dollars for, (this is some pricey bird song!). I spoke to one guy who told me that he'd just bought a couple of birds for $600 each, with another one of his birds setting him back $1,800! The main type of bird that you see here is the zebra dove, native to Southeast Asia. Men come early in the morning and hoist their birds in their fine cages up onto the poles. A social club more than anything, the guys come here to chat, gossip and while away their time (most are retired). The best time to visit is Sunday 9.30am to noon.

🏠 Block 159, Ang Mo Kio Ave 5, 560156

🚌 Yio Chu Kang

📘 Kebun Baru Birdsinging Club

🕐 Mon – Sun 9am - 5pm

Sungei Buloh Wetland Reserve

9 *Wildlife Wonder*

In the northwest of Singapore, a stone's throw from Malaysia, looking out over the Straits of Johor, is the fascinating nature reserve at Sungei Buloh. With it being famous for its estuary saltwater crocodiles, you can hope to spot these snappy creatures as you stand on the bridge and peer down into the water. Observe monitor lizards and tortoises swimming in the ponds, as well as blue-spotted mudskippers poking out of holes. It is a popular place for bird watching, so bring binoculars to look closely at the migratory birds on their way to Australia, as well as herons, kingfishers and sunbirds. Wander along the boardwalks and spot huge spiders making spindly webs in the trees. A good option for a half-day trip, it's around 30 minutes' drive from city centre. Do note that public transport isn't great up in this area.

🏠 301 Neo Tiew Cres, 718925

🚇 Kranji

🔦 nparks.gov.sg

📷 @nparksbuzz

🕐 Mon – Sun 7am – 7pm

Bollywood Veggies

10 *Tropical Garden*

Way up north in the Kranji countryside, where goat and vegetable farms still survive, a secret garden exists, providing a rustic contrast to the city. Spend a morning here walking around the carefully nurtured rows of banana trees, fragrant flowers, and gorgeous greenery. There are sections such as 'butterfly dreams' with flowers purposely planted to attract these pretty creatures, as well as an 'insect hotel'. Head to the kitchen garden to find capsicum, laksa leaves, basil and oregano growing. They run interesting tours such as the 'medicine women talk' where you walk through the Bollywood Nature Pharmacy and learn about ancient Malay and Javanese plant remedies. Similar to the Sungei Buloh Wetlands, Bollywood Veggies isn't the easiest place to get to, and is best reached by taxi.

🏠 100 Neo Tiew Rd, 719026

🚉 Kranji

☎ +65 68985001

🖈 bollywoodveggies.com

🕐 Wed - Fri 9.30am - 6.30pm
Sat - Sun 8am - 6.30pm
Closed Mon - Tues (except PH)

Pulau Ubin

11 *Kampung-Style Island*

It's super fun to get on a quick 'bum boat' ride from the east side of Singapore across to Pulau Ubin, known as, 'the island that time forgot'. A throwback to local life in the 1960s, this lush little island is covered with trees and lakes, has original kampung villages, and is home to wildlife such as native wild boar, hornbill birds and long-tailed macaques. Once you arrive, rent a mountain bike to explore the hilly terrain on bike trails that wind through beautiful mangroves that leads to a stunning coastal boardwalk. Discreetly located off a sidetrack is the fascinating Buddhist temple, Wei Tuo Fa Gong, and during your exploration, also look out for the eerie German Girl Shrine. Finish off the day with a couple of Chang beers at the local beachside restaurants on the island before heading back to the mainland.

🏠 Pulau Ubin, 508329
(depart from Changi Point
Ferry Teminal, 499172)

🖱 nparks.gov.sg

📷 @nparksbuzz

🕐 Boats to and from Pulau Ubin
operate from sunrise to sunset

Priscilla Shunmugam

Taking the surnames from Priscilla's Chinese mother and Indian father, Ong Shunmugam is the epitome of a modern Singaporean label fiercely proud of its Asian heritage. Originally making her mark on the local fashion scene by reintroducing a contemporary version of the Chinese cheongsam dress, her pieces weave in stories from history, taking influences from Japanese kimonos to Indonesian batik with a nod towards the fading Singapore Peranakan culture.

The Fashion Designer

An Interview with Priscilla Shunmugam

I went to meet Priscilla at the Ong Shunmugam flagship store on Jalan Merah Saga, in the Holland Village neighbourhood. Like everything Priscilla does with her brand, the store is carefully thought out, with every corner created to tell a story. Most interestingly, at the back of the store there is a large window looking into the on-site atelier, where busy seamstresses work away on new pieces, alongside rolls of rich fabrics lining the walls sourced from travels around Asia. In another part of the shop, I spotted one of the girls experimenting with stitching bits of embroidery onto a pair of white Vans trainers, in preparation for a collaboration with the skatewear brand. On the rails, pieces in the collection include a sari-cheongsam, a design merging traditional Indian and Chinese wear, where a sari sash is connected to cheongsam, a design created to cater to the increasing number of mixed-race marriages, whereby the bride is able to represent both cultures in her choice of clothing. We sat on a sofa at the front of the shop, opposite a wall of personal photos of Priscilla's respective Indian and Chinese families, with a large black plaque with gold Chinese characters above them that translates into 'To Glorify Your Ancestors', a gift from her family.

Tell me about how you started the fashion label Ong Shunmugam?

We started the label in December 2010 and it's been a fast uphill journey since then. It has luckily been mostly high points, rather than low points which is unusual, but it's certainly been very challenging. We've had to learn along the way, and at the same time challenge many assumptions and restrictions when it comes to developing and running a fashion label in Singapore.

You originally trained as a lawyer. How did you make the leap from the world of law to starting your own business?

It was a matter of just deciding to do it, rather than to keep thinking about it. When you want to make a change, especially when it requires a certain degree of risk taking, sometimes overthinking it can leave you in the same position, so I stopped thinking and I decided to do.

Did travelling overseas influence your decision to change your career path, or would you have made this change if you were in Singapore?

I don't think that it would have happened if I was living here, because there aren't the right channels for somebody like me to explore that kind of switch. I was in London, but I could have been in New York or Paris, and the same thing would have sparked. It was mainly about being at that point of time in my life where I was hoping to change.

What gave you the idea to start a fashion brand steeped in Southeast Asian heritage?

It hadn't been done before, and fashion was sort of neglected in this region. Fashion has very good representation in North America, South America, Western Europe, and increasingly in Eastern Europe – but you can safely say that Southeast Asia is very underrepresented. It's a sad situation because there is a lot of history and heritage when it comes to textiles and costumes here. You go to every single Southeast Asian country and they have their own type of fabric, their own kinds of costumes or traditional outfits, but it's never really been bought into the 21st century. I felt like this was an area that was worth talking about.

Do you feel a responsibility to tell these Asian stories in an authentic way that reflects your own heritage?

Yes. It didn't really start out that way, but it has evolved into that because the deeper you dig, and the more research that you do, you realise that the reason why it's neglected is simply because either no one is interested or no one is really capable. It felt like a duty to take on this job, because it didn't feel like anyone else was keen.

Can you tell me about some of your travel experiences when you've sourced fabrics from around Asia?

We can't just go to the tourist spots to source, so that means that we leave the cities, and go further out to the villages to really uncover the gems – that's usually where the adventure lies. Sometimes you're in areas where English is not spoken and likewise you don't speak the native language, so you have to rely on sign language, as well as getting over distrust and unfamiliarity. These are all recipes for disaster or adventure, but I usually survive it. I think it's nice, because in these places, when they meet an adventurer it's typically a Caucasian person. They don't normally see Asians themselves showing an interest, so it's a nice reaction. It's not animosity; it's more of "why would you be interested?" The furthest north we've been is China, and the furthest south is Sri Lanka – we've covered everywhere in between.

You are Indian Chinese, from Malaysia and now living and working in Singapore – how does your multicultural background influence your ideas, your life and your work?

It is certainly influential and very helpful as a creative person to have such a wide reservoir of influences from which to draw from. For someone else who isn't able to tap into this, it can either be overwhelming or confusing, and you sometimes run the risk of diluting, or not being able to focus. I've always been raised with a multi-perspective, which makes me more sensitive. I'm very used to that situation of feeling like the outsider, but at the same like the insider. Feeling like a minority but at the same time a majority. Relativity is more and more important in the 21st century in this very borderless world. I like to look at fashion from a very inclusive point of view, as opposed to exclusive. For example, a French couture label or a Japanese ceramics specialist – these are very exclusive perspectives and there's nothing wrong with that, but it's nice to have an alternative which says, "we care about everybody and we are for everybody".

In terms of fashion, Western brands dominate in Singapore. Do you think that there will be a time when Singaporean and Asian brands will be recognised globally?

Realistically it's a challenge, simply because the way the global fashion industry and economy works is still very tilted in their favour. Trends, industry norms, the big decisions are still made in the West and I don't think that it's going to change at all, so we have to accept that. But at the same time, the one change that is happening is where consumers are speaking with their credit cards. The spending power is in the East. Once upon a time Western brands, or any brand for that matter, would have paid attention to the Western consumer, the usual markets, and the usual big, top-tier cities. These days that attention has clearly shifted to Asia. What has changed is that you can still have decisions being made in the West, but they will be based on the Asian consumer.

If you are an Asian designer, the obvious upper hand you have is the fact that you know this area better than anyone else, so you can literally draw a very straight line from brand to consumer, from maker to owner. We realised that right from day one. We know that this is clearly something that we have under our belt. The real challenge for a brand like ours is - who is the customer? Who is the priority? Is it still the Western consumer or is it the Asian consumer, or is it both?

Have you noticed a change in local consumers wanting to not only buy Western brands, but Asian brands too?

At least 70% of the reason why we are successful is simply because the Asian consumer today is a very different creature. The Asian woman in particular (since we do womenswear) is a very educated, exposed, confident, well-travelled and well-equipped consumer. Sometimes she has more spending power than many consumers in the West so if you are an Asian brand that can speak their language, and I don't mean literally but I mean their design language, their cultural language, their heritage language, you can stand to win their loyalty, and I think that's what's happening. It's not to say that they're not patronising their favourite Western brands, that's still happening, but now they can finally have a bit of variety in their wardrobe, when once upon a time they couldn't. They could but they had to rely on very literal, dumb-down translations. If you go to Chinatown and you look at the kind of cheongsams or souvenirs that you can get, it's usually very reductive, it's cheap, it's tacky, and it's a caricature. That's never been something that an Asian woman today can accept so easily, because for her she thinks, "I don't want that". We try to offer a slightly more thoughtful alternative, and that's what's working.

You mention that in the West there is a clichéd view of the East - can you give me more of your thoughts on this?

It's not really anybody's fault. In Asia, we haven't yet got to the stage where we are inclusive enough, or accessible enough in terms of how we present or articulate ourselves. For example, if you go to a bookshop and try to find a book that can explain the evolution of Singaporean design and creativity, you'd be hard pressed to find something that could give you a balanced, non-top-down government written, government endorsed book. You can't have that when you're looking for robust, objective discourse, arguments and perspectives. When there's a lack of that, who is going take that role - it's Western academics, scholars, and industry experts. They've got to come up with their own books and research papers, and when that happens, it's very natural to make assumptions, because information is not readily made available to them. It's nobody's fault, that's the way it is. In the West I find that there are naturally a lot of assumptions being made, which are usually based on stereotypes or from looking at things from a far, say, sitting in an office in Berlin; that's how it's done. Or when they do come to Asia, there are just too many layers to cut through to get to the truth.

    As Asians, we are not raised to speak, argue or share – these are not inherently Asian concepts. It's going to take time, and it's going to take effort, really from us more than from anyone else, because we need to be able to speak, share and open our doors so that people can learn more, and we can reduce that misunderstanding and misconception of what Asia really is. That's where the current generation of Asian creatives becomes important. The more I see, the more I can't just run a fashion label and do designs, I need to send out a very clear message whether it's through research, publications, giving talks or sharing knowledge.

Where do you go for inspiration?

When I travel and source, that definitely helps, but most of the time my inspiration comes from reading books. Sometimes in order to look forwards you have to look backwards, and that's very much the design philosophy for us. It's about looking within and trying to create something from that.

What do you love most about Singapore?

Singapore has been very fair to a foreigner like me (Priscilla is from Malaysia). It's been my home for 15 years now, but from the moment I arrived here, all I have received is opportunity and equality. I've never been made to feel like an outsider, nor have I ever been made to feel like I need to conform or to become anyone else different. In many other parts of the world you can't always feel that sense of freedom. I know it doesn't rank highly in terms of personal liberties or press freedoms and I'm fully aware of that, but in my experience I've had nothing but possibilities.

 ongshunmugam.com

@ongshunmugam

Aik Beng Chia

Aik Beng Chia, or ABC as he is known, starting capturing everyday scenes in Singapore after buying an iPhone 2G in 2008. Zooming in on the daily lives of the people he sees on the streets, ABC's photos are a much-admired alternative to the polished, modern imagery of the city. Whether he's shooting regulars at Heap Seng Leong coffee shop or recording the public mourning of Singapore's first Prime Minister, Lee Kuan Yew, ABC's photography portfolio is a genuine refection of his country.

The Street Photographer

An Interview with Aik Beng Chia

I went to meet Aik Beng Chia down a noisy alleyway off a side road in Chinatown behind the old Chinese Restaurant Yum Cha, during his lunch break. A couple of red plastic chairs are propped up against the wall with unfinished cups of black kopi left on the tables. A loud lorry parks up and a man offloads big blue cylinders of gas that clang into each other as they are being delivered to the kitchens in this busy cluster. I can tell that this is where one of Singapore's most respected street photographers feels most at home. Not in a quiet, clean, contemporary cafe, but hanging out in the gritty streets, rubbing shoulders with everyday Singaporean folk.

Tell me about your background and what made you get started in photography?

I work as a designer and a photographer for an advertising firm (BBH). Apart from day-to-day design work, I help out with in-house photography projects for corporates and for the company. I started to do my own photography when I first got my iPhone, which was back in 2008. I used my phone because I couldn't afford a proper camera. It was only in 2010 that I decided to be more focused with what I wanted to do. I felt that there was a need to record what I see on an everyday basis, of everyday Singapore scenes, because as we all know, Singapore is constantly changing. Landscape-wise, nothing lasts forever.

My favourite genre is street photography. I prefer to shoot the older generation, the pioneer generation, because I feel that they played such an important role in the building of this nation. They went through World War II and the Independence. To me, these types of characters are more appealing, because in my day job I look at models all the time. I look at pretty things all the time; everything is perfect. I am more into the gritty side, because to me, Singapore isn't just one-dimensional. The side that is being shown to the world is the postcard side of Singapore. There are many facets, and I try to cover that.

Which photographers do you particularly admire, and have influenced your work?

I am inspired a lot by Japanese photographers, such as Jun Abe. His style is considered to be like the black and white version of Alex Webb, the Magnum photographer, who uses colour and lots of layers. He documents the everyday life of people whom he comes across, and not only people but also things in general, like still life and architecture.

In terms of how I frame my composition, I am actually inspired by the cinema and the work of Wong Kar-wai (Hong Kong filmmaker) and Christopher Doyle (Australian cinematographer). Christopher Doyle shot a lot of films for Wong Kar-wai like '*In the Mood for Love*' and '*Chungking Express*'. In terms of composition that's where I get my source of inspiration, it's from watching movies.

What first drew you to street photography?

Street photography is harder. It's more challenging because you can't plan and you can't stage. I prefer that instant, spontaneous moment when it just happens in front of you. I'm not into trying to capture a certain moment, or what Henri Cartier-Bresson (French photographer) would call 'a decisive moment'. I am more interested in everyday life. It can be a very simple shot, it can be a very mundane thing, but to me it holds a meaning. When I photograph it, I hope that the viewer will ask questions.

A lot of my photos have a double meaning, because they relate to what I am going through or what I am seeing right now, based on the current situation that's happening all over the world.

For example, I was walking on the pavement and I saw something on the grass, so I went up close and there was a passport photo of a person, but it was covered by a broken identity card. I shot it because it represents the struggle with our own identity. It can be as simple as that. Someone just threw something away yet it can represent a more profound kind of meaning.

Rochor Centre

If it inspires people or makes them feel something, then I think it's a memorable one. It doesn't need to be technically perfect. For me, it happens very randomly. I walk a lot. I don't look for images; I let the images come to me. I tend to get lost all the time, because I don't want to plan where I go. It's like what they say about Daidō Moriyama (Japanese photographer); he's like a dog, he just wanders like a stray dog.

What cameras do you like to shoot with?

I mainly use my mobile phone and a compact camera. I don't really like bigger cameras because when it comes to handling the gear, I'm not that technically inclined. I like my camera to be very simple, compact and easy to use, so I don't have to spend time adjusting the settings. I've been called a hit and run shooter. It has to be fast. I previously did a series where I go up-close to a face and I snap and walk away. Hit and run.

How important is it for you to document your home country?

When I started with photography, I always envied my friends that got to travel abroad to take beautiful images. Then one day I met the founder of Invisible Photographer Asia, Kevin WY Lee. He said, "What's wrong with shooting Singapore? If you can't photograph Singapore then what makes you so sure you can photograph other cities? You have to start somewhere and what better place than your own backyard, because it is where you are most familiar". I spent the next four to five years shooting solely in Singapore, until only recently where I got the opportunity to travel to other cities. What I do in Singapore applies to Tokyo, Hong Kong or Bangkok. I still apply the hit and run technique.

What do you love most about Singapore?

What I love most is that it's a multicultural city. There are a lot of different festivals and customs from each culture, which creates its own uniqueness and flavour. Singapore is one of those cities where you can see so many races from all over the world at one time. If you want to see Koreans, Europeans or Chinese, you go to the tourist spots. If you want to see locals, you go to the heartland.

Singapore is always projecting a clean image. I wish certain parts of it could still remain so that the future generations can see it with their own eyes, rather than on some multimedia presentation. For me, I like to smell the street; I can sit here next to the dump - that's what the street is all about.

Changi Beach

What are you most proud of as a Singaporean?

I'm blessed with a country that is still quite safe. Especially for someone like me who goes out in the middle of the night to shoot, I don't have to worry about being mugged. No country is perfect. Every city has its good and its bad, and the same goes for Singapore. But what I am proud of is the ability to move about without fear.

Where are your favourite places to shoot in Singapore?

I prefer to go to the heartland estates. That's where you get to see the other side of Singapore life, the local scenes. I like to go to places like Jurong, Yishun, Woodlands or Redhill. Tiong Bahru is also quite interesting because it's got charm.

In the heartlands, I prefer to go to the wet markets and the food centres because that's where you see everyone – everyone is there, doing their groceries. For tourist spots, I go to Chinatown, Little India or Arab Street.

Can you tell me about some of your favourite projects you have worked on in Singapore?

I like photographing the Lao Sai Tao Yuan Teochew Opera Troupe. Even though it's been shot to death, I feel that it's very important because there aren't many of them left, and the new generation isn't so interested in this sort of thing. I think that it's very important to try and keep it alive through photography.

Other than that, it's the everyday life. I did a project called 'Passing', looking at people on an escalator. When I commute, I started to observe that everyone has very different expressions, and most of them are either glued to their phone, or thinking about something - some are happy, some are sad, some are troubled. I try to capture all these emotions. My question is - how often do you get to look at the expression of the person opposite you? It's amazing; some of them are picking their nose, scratching, or doing little gestures - it really reflects so much.

For a visitor wanting to get a real sense of Singapore, where do you suggest they go?

The heartlands. Take the train and travel all over. Most of the estates have a main station, so it's easy, you can hop around. This is what I do, and what I tell my overseas friends who have never been to Singapore before to do. I say, come; let's take a train. It's the first thing we do.

aikbengchia.com

@aikbengchia

Rivervale Street

Compassvale Road

Violet Oon

Violet Oon is considered by many to be one of the leading authorities on Asian cuisine, having written about food professionally early on in her career, to opening up her own restaurants which she runs today. Violet is part of the Peranakan culture, a Singaporean Nyonya, with a blend of heritages from native Malay and Chinese immigrants who came to the Malay Archipelago for trade. She enthusiastically shares the flavours of Nyonya food, bringing the cuisine from her home to the public.

The Chef

An Interview with Violet Oon

I went to meet Violet Oon at her namesake restaurant, National Kitchen by Violet Oon, located at the National Gallery Singapore, overlooking the Padang. Violet was born into a colonial lifestyle in the late 1940s, became a food journalist in the 1970s and opened up her first food outlet in the 1990s - each portion of her life reflected in the restaurant through both the food and style of the space. The walls are a treasure trove of memories and snapshots in time, from the photos of the first soy sauce factory in Singapore, to personal family photos of entertaining at home. The smell of spices floats from the kitchen, a medley of signature Southeast Asian scents.

How did you get started on your food journey?

I first learnt the art and skills of Nyonya cuisine at the age of 16, when I took lessons from my aunts, my father's sisters. They were the ones that carried on the heritage of the cuisine from our ancestors. In Singapore, my mother was liberated - she was a secretary and a career woman, and did not learn the nuances of this type of cooking. In those days, you were not meant to be a superwoman, so if you were a secretary, you did not do the housework.

My first teachers were my aunt, Mrs Nona Bong and my great aunt by marriage, Mrs Nanny Khoo. I also learnt in the traditional Asian way from Sifus (masters), who come from a long line of family chefs and cooks, and teach the next generation to carry the torch. My first cooking classes were in Singapore in 1965-1966. My aunts didn't have proper recipes, but they were very accurate, because they were cooking everyday. Recipes used to be written in five cents of this, three cents of that and one cent of this, so that makes no sense 30 years later! So I asked my aunts to show me, and I would write as they cooked. I then got very good at estimating the measurements, such as how many teaspoons and tablespoons went into the dishes. When you actually watch people cooking, it is different from a recipe.

How did you become a chef?

Cooking and becoming a chef happened by chance. I started off my career as a journalist in 1971, becoming the arts and music critic and features writer in the now defunct newspaper called the New Nation.

I then started writing about food in 1974 - my editor David Kraal said, "We had better have someone who can cook to write about food".

During my career as a food journalist in the 1970s to the late 1990s, chefs would open their kitchens and invite me to cook with them. I visited professional chefs in restaurants in Singapore (doing French, German, Italian, Chinese and Malay cuisine) and also abroad to places such as New Orleans, Paris, London, Australia and Hong Kong. In this way, a lot of my cooking skills came by observation and osmosis. The experiences that were of particular value to me though was when I was invited into kitchens in homes, where I would see each families' own particular interpretation of well-loved dishes.

On the international food scene in the 1980s and 1990s there was a whole generation of highly respected women chefs who did not go through training in culinary schools, or who did not rise up the culinary ladder through working in hotel or restaurant kitchens, including Julia Child and Alice Waters from America, and Maggie Beer and Stephanie Alexander from Australia. You could say I became a chef in the same way as these women did, by starting with a love and abiding interest and dedication to the art and craft of cooking a particular cuisine, and then sharing it with other people.

Can you explain more about Peranakan culture and Nyonya food?

Peranakan culture is a marriage of the East and East with a strong dose of the West. Starting with the native Malay culture in Malacca and Penang and finally in Singapore, where Chinese male immigrants married Malay maidens.

My culture, that of the Peranakans, evolved more than five centuries ago, with the flourishing of trade between China and the Malay Peninsula, although it started to die out from the 1970s. It seemed as though there were very few of us, mainly concentrated in the Katong area of Singapore, which today is still the heartland of the Peranakan culture. Having been born in Singapore and brought up for much of my childhood in Malacca, I was very in touch with the essence of Peranakan life, with their specific art, music, food and dress. In the 1950s living in Malacca, I saw a world from a past age. For example, there were multi-generational families living in mini-apartments in courtyard houses, family dinners where the men ate first and wives and daughters last, and women who dressed in opulent, richly embroidered kebayas over hand-painted sarong skirts from Pekalongan in Indonesia. Yet coming from a modern Peranakan family, we were more in tune with the 20th century than of the past, and I did not quite live the life of a Peranakan. At home, we did not speak Peranakan patois, ate both Chinese Hokkien home cooking as well as Peranakan dishes and Western food. My mother did not dress the way Peranakan women did in their sarong kebayas, choosing instead to wear modern dress and the Chinese cheongsam.

Peranakan food is very strongly Malay based with the addition of Chinese Hokkien dishes. The Chinese originators of the culture came from the Fujian Province in China, and so the Chinese part of cuisine is Hokkien – a lot of dark soya sauces, taucheo, garlic and shallots. Indians, who came from Southern India, bought with them their curries and rich aromatic seed spices which added to the cuisine, as well as a strong touch of British cooking which you'll see in the cakes and morning breakfasts.

What are your favourite Nyonya dishes?

A few of my favourite dishes are:

Kuay Pie Tee (also known as 'top hat')
Julienned bamboo shoot and turnip poached in a prawn bisque served in a deep fried 'top hat' cup topped with prawn, chilli sauce and a sweet fruit sauce.

Ngoh Hiang
Deep fried prawn, crab and chicken with water chestnut seasoned with five-spice powder wrapped in bean curd skin.

Beef Rendang
A creamy and spicy Nyona dish with Malay and Indonesian Padang cuisine origins. Tender beef shin braised with spices of galangal, shallots, ginger, garlic, belacan (shrimp paste) and chillies. It has a Malay bouquet with turmeric leaf, kaffir lime leaf, and local bay leaves (daun salam).

Do you have a favourite ingredient?

The combination made in heaven is the marriage of coconut milk and gula melaka (palm sugar). For savoury flavours, essential ingredients include galangal, turmeric, lemongrass, shallots, chilies and belacan.

Where do you go for inspiration?

I'm inspired by home cooking. My whole childhood was spent going to my aunts' and different people's homes. What you eat at home with your family is a reflection of your life and your family's life, your travels, and where you have been. For example, Anglo Indians have a unique food, which is neither Indian, nor English.

I'm fascinated by dishes or recipes that are locked in time. The food, as well as drinks that would have gone with it, represents a certain time and place. I was born in 1949, so in my restaurant there are these different layers of time. These dishes are like archaeological records. The restaurant is the brainchild of my two children, but for them, it's also about capturing and remembering the family cooking.

How important do you think food is to the Singaporean culture and identity?

It's very important, more so in the last few years, as people start to question what is dying off, such as the hawker culture. It's so essential to our psyche, more so than people realise, because expenditure on food here is much higher than in other cultures. A lot of disposable income goes into food. Food seems to be the tie that binds us culturally and emotionally as a people, much more so than a shared history of art or music or dance or literature.

What other chefs in Singapore do you admire?

I like what Willin Low, chef of *Wild Rocket* (p124) does. In the end, it doesn't matter what cuisine you do, the test is whether it tastes good. He has taken a lot of traditional flavours from his culture (Singaporean), which is different from mine, and reworked it. It's all very delicious, and not only delicious but cooked properly technically.

But I'm more concerned with eating local hawker food that is very old, and sooner or later, the people running the hawker stalls are going to retire and nobody's going to be able to eat their food. It's scary.

Which restaurants do you most enjoy eating at on your day off?

For nostalgia and old-fashioned authentic tastes, I love the Ngoh Hiang at *China Street Fritters* in Maxwell Food Centre. They are the last in the whole of Singapore for what they do. The food wouldn't even taste the same as if you tried it in China, as they came over 70 years ago, so their cooking style has evolved. I want to be able to savour flavours and textures that may die off within the next generation. Already, many old-school hawkers have closed their shutters due to the extreme hard work it takes to cook authentic, old-fashioned food as well as the high cost of employing kitchen helpers.

I love the pau at *Teck Kee Tanglin Pau* and at *Tiong Bahru Pau* (p48). To me that's the real Singapore texture. The Singapore pau pastry and the Hong Kong style pau pastry are very different, for instance, when you go to the tim sum restaurants in Hong Kong, there's a very fluffy texture. I want to see places like *Teck Kee* preserved. It's interesting because it's truly Singaporean. This type of food originally came from China, but now they use a particular recipe and a particular style that doesn't exist in Hong Kong. Those are the things that I want to see and I want people to know, not whether somebody cooks very well, but whether these nuances are kept. At *Tiong Bahru Pau*, that's the actual Singapore texture and Singapore dough, but how many people know that? I would love to see this texture and dough preserved. It's very important.

I would like to see the children of the old hawkers take over. They grew up watching their fathers cooking these dishes for 20 years, so there's a certain osmosis and DNA which is so difficult to capture. You can't teach it. There are things that they know, that they don't even realise that they know. You may be able to cook the food excellently as a new chef, but there are certain touches, which you would only have if you grew up with it.

What do you love most about Singapore?

I love our inclusiveness, and our unique Singlish multi-cultural sense of humour; our classic put-downs that speak a volume in a word or two. I love our whole natural environment. Our urban jungle is literally a jungle with lots of plants, trees and foliage. I love our built and unbuilt environment.

Singapore has much more character than people think. What I find very funny is that a lot of westerners coming to the Far East think that exotic means dirty. If it's dirty, then it's exotic. They can't believe that it can be clean and have character. You just have to go to any of the HDB areas and just hangout.

I also love the diversity. It's got a bit of Britain here, a bit of India there; it's got a bit of everything.

What are you most proud of as a Singaporean?

I think what makes me most proud is our inclusiveness, which is now the more obvious in the midst of non-inclusiveness in many societies. A mosque will be next to a temple, which is next to a church. To us, religious tolerance and racial harmony is so important, for example, in the schools, children celebrate a racial harmony day. Regarding our respect for each other's religion, customs and sense of private cultural space, although we may not be the best at this in the world, we can be proud of what we are and where we are.

violetoon.com

@violetoonsingapore

Listening to Mukesh

by Pooja Nansi

Driving to your block,
I slide in my father's cassette
of old Hindi songs and
I am humming in twilight
to the legendary
playback singer's baritone
releasing those sounds in that
language that makes me feel like I am
home. In the back of my throat,
I can taste my grandmother's
translucent thin chappatis
that as children we would
hold up
to the light,
the dough so evenly rolled out
by her hands that not
one lump would show.
I never appreciated them till her hands
shook so much,
she could no longer grip
the rolling pin.

I hear the children from the slum
that emerged behind my grandparents small
two-storey apartment block.
They are swearing
in that deliciously punctuated rhythm
only the born-and-bred tongue
can dance to.

I am home for a while.
I can smell dust and kerosene
in the air and hear
high-pitched devotions to the gods
blending without objection
into the stone thud bass
of the latest film song.

Jamming my brakes at a traffic light,
I realise home is supposed to be these
dustless streets and the smells
are alien culinary concoctions,
like pigs' knuckles and chicken anatomy,
that my migrant tastebuds
cannot migrate towards.
I have taught my tongue
to like the garlic sting
of Hainanese chili paste
and form some Hokkien curse words.
It even enjoys the harsh bite of it,
but it is not
a taste, a language
that makes my heart sing
like these notes on my
car stereo.

Jaoon kaha batayen dil,
Duniya badi hain sangdil
Chandini Aiyen Ghar Jalane
Sujhe Na Koyi Manzil.

Tell me where I should go
in a world filled with indifference.
The moonlight filters into my house,
But I do not belong,
neither can I think of a destination.

Pooja Nansi is the author of two collections of poetry, the co-editor of an anthology of Singaporean poetry and the co-author of a teacher's resource for Singaporean poetry. Since April 2013, she has been curating a monthly spoken word and poetry showcase called Speakeasy.

↖ poojanansi.com

"Imaginary Geographies of the Singapore Heartland"
by Ann Ang

A: So you think Jurong now is better than Singapore last time?

23: Ok lah, I think is okay.

A: Why, Uncle?

23: Got enough space, flats far apart. You don't see directly into people's house, but you can still see them walking downstairs, so you know who they are.

A: So you think Jurong is better than other parts of Singapore?

23: Yah! Better, better than those congested places East-side. All those lorongs, you drive a car also cannot drive properly. Those were the places which the government fail to clean up...lorong 23, lorong 15.

A: So Uncle, you got go there?

23: No lah, why I go to such dirty places?

A: You sure or not, Uncle?

23: Yah! Those places are not normal. You want to cross road got no traffic light, the buildings don't have number, the shop don't have name, unless you know the people, and since I don't know them, they treat me like dirt lidat.

A: So how?

23: Just knock down everything lah.

A: Like Jurong last time?

23: Jurong is new, when Jurong got flats—all this is new land, new place, all good, no problem, no ghost.

Excerpt from *Bang My Car* by Ann Ang

Ann Ang's poetry, fiction and non-fiction have appeared in various publications and journals. The second edition of her Singlish-English collection of short stories, *Bang My Car*, is published by Math Paper Press and is available from Books Actually.

overheard at al-azhar
by Joshua Ip

"one egg, one kosong". "same." "then drinks?" "teh si
siu dai". "one milo peng". "eh, work mainland
good ornot?" "like that lor. luckily
last time got bia cheena, then now still can.

you got hear ang moh speak chinese before?
the words correct, but accent cmi...
then how to win someone from Singapore?
lifelong challenge, maciam lky.

next time, they also start from primary one
then do the ting xie zhao ju zuo wen shit
then everybody also mother tongue
but still got years before they can make it."

the prata is served by prc
no one notices, since it's crispy

Excerpt from *Sonnets from the Singlish* by Joshua Ip

Joshua Ip is a poet, editor, and literary organiser. He is the author of three
volumes of poetry: *sonnets from the singlish upsize edition* (威力加强版) (2015),
making love with scrabble tiles (2013), and *sonnets from the singlish* (2012),
published by Math Paper Press and available from Books Actually.

 joshuaip.com

LOST GUIDES
LOVES

Coolest Coffee Spot
Chye Seng Huat Hardware

Must See Indie Movies
The Projector

Day Trip
Pulau Ubin

Drinking Den
Operation Dagger

Authentic Asian Fashion
Ong Shunmugam

BBQ
Burnt Ends

Local Food Feast
Old Airport Road Food Centre

Brilliant Bookshop
BooksActually

Vintage & Antique Furniture
Junkie's Corner

Inspiring Art
Singapore Art Museum

My Singapore Travel Notes

Date	Location	Notes

Date	Location	Notes

Date	Location	Notes

Date	Location	Notes

Date	Location	Notes

Acknowledgements

Lost Guides - Singapore was proudly crowdfunded by 141 lovely people who helped me to raise $6,173 USD, which went towards the production of the book. (You can check out my crowdfunding page and watch the video on indiegogo.com/at/lostguidessingapore).

A big thank you to everyone that contributed towards my crowdfunding goal and helped me make this book a reality.

Patrons

Alex Ottignon, Alex Preston-Morley, Alfred Waring, Alice Danilovich, Babak Ghatineh, Ben Ainley, Benedict Taylor, Benyna Richards, Camilla Lindberg Christensen, Caspar Chittenden, Catherine Adamson, Charles Bennie Danielle Pereira, Harry Gabb, Holly O'Keeffe, Jeremy Martin, Jeremy Muller, Jerome Steele, Katy Beechey, Lisa Langstrom, Lisa Smith. Lynman Woo, Michelle Edmunds, Michelle Lim, Nee Yeoh, Peter Melrose, Rebecca Smith, Rosamund Chittenden, Sabrina Nguyen, Shahla Ghatineh, Simren Priestley, Sophie Williamson, Tara Thivolet, Thao Le

Thank you to all those that joined me with the exploration side of the project, as well as those that gave me their tips, and shared their Singapore secrets with me. Thanks to everyone who gave me their advice, shared their knowledge, and donated their time and skills to help me to put this book into your hands.

Additional photography:

Cheek by Jowl	Atlas - EK Yap
Employees Only	Meatsmith Little India
Native Bar	Ong Shunmugam
The Spiffy Dapper	Aik Beng Chia